PERSONALITY

Books by the Author

The Psychoanalysis of Symptoms

Dictionary of Psychopathology

Group Psychotherapy and Personality: Intersecting Structures

Sleep Disorders: Insomnia and Narcolepsy

The 4 Steps to Peace of Mind: The Simple Effective Way to Cure Our Emotional Symptoms (Romanian edition, 2008; Japanese edition, 2011)

Love Is Not Enough: What It Takes to Make It Work

Haggadah: A Passover Seder for the Rest of Us

Greedy, Cowardly, and Weak: Hollywood's Jewish Stereotypes

Hollywood Movies on the Couch: A Psychoanalyst Examines 15 Famous Films

The Discovery of God: A Psycho/Evolutionary Perspective

The Making of Ghosts: A Novel

A Consilience of Natural and Social Sciences: A Memoir of Original Contributions

Books Coauthored (with Anthony Burry, Ph. D.)

Psychopathology and Differential Diagnosis: A Primer
Volume 1. *History of Psychopathology*
Volume 2. *Diagnostic Primer*

Handbook of Psychodiagnostic Testing: Analysis of Personality in the Psychological Report (four English editions; Japanese edition, 2011)

Books Edited

Group Cohesion: Theoretical and Clinical Perspectives

The Nightmare: Psychological and Biological Foundations

Books Coedited (with Robert Plutchik, Ph. D.)

Emotion: Theory, Research, and Experience (volumes 1-5):
Volume 1: *Theories of Emotion;* Volume 2: *Emotions in Early Development;*
Volume 3: *Biological Foundations of Emotion;* Volume 4: *The Measurement of Emotion;* Volume 5: *Emotion, Psychopathology, and Psychotherapy*

PERSONALITY

How It Forms

Henry Kellerman, Ph.D.

2012

AMHF
AMERICAN
MENTAL
HEALTH
FOUNDATION
BOOKS

American Mental Health Foundation Inc
Post Office Box 3
Riverdale, NY 10471-0003

Printed in the United States of America

americanmentalhealthfoundation.org

Library of Congress Cataloging-in-Publication Data

Kellerman, Henry.
Personality : how it forms / Henry Kellerman.
p. cm.
ISBN 978-1-59056-353-3 (pbk. : alk. paper) —
ISBN 978-1-59056-354-0 (ebook)
1. Personality. I. Title.
BF698. K365 2012
155.2—dc23
              2011049260

All identifying information in the case histories discussed
has been omitted to the extent that this has been possible.

**In memory of
Alex Kupperblatt**

My buddy, Al.
The charismatic Navy man, who captained:
Velli; Kaye's Navy; and, Vanilla.

Here's to:

Movie lines; Stanbrook; Sammy's Romanian;
Caribbean jaunts; Montauk; Caravana Club Pachangas;
and, 40 years of laughing.

Contents

Publisher's Foreword

As the present book is issued, The American Mental Health Foundation celebrates nearly ninety years of work. Organized in 1924, AMHF is dedicated to the welfare of people suffering from emotional problems, with a particular concern for the emotional issues of individuals with special needs and elders. For many years, AMHF generally devoted its efforts to bettering quality of treatment and developing more effective methods, available also to lower-income wage earners.

The major therapeutic advances and improved training methods are described in the existing publications: the three-part series The Search for the Future. Two of these books are available on our Web site under the titles *The Challenge for Group Psychotherapy* (volume 1) and *The Challenge for Psychoanalysis and Psychotherapy: Solutions for the Future* (volume 2). Portions of these books are also reprinted on the AMHF Web site in French and German, for those segments of the international community. Volume 3, originally published in 2000 by Prometheus, is now available from AMHF Books: *Crucial Choices – Crucial Changes: The Resurrection of Psychotherapy.*

Under the supervision and direction of Dr. William Van Ornum, AMHF Books is an exciting new venture. Begun in 2009, this publishing program now numbers seven important works on violence and stress by Dr. Raymond B. Flannery Jr., one of the foremost experts on posttraumatic stress disorder (PTSD). It also includes four titles by Erich Fromm: reprints of two classics, *The Revolution of Hope* and *The Heart of Man,* as well as two posthumous books, *Beyond Freud* and *The Pathology of Normalcy.*

The present volume, by psychologist and psychoanalyst Dr. Henry Kellerman, is an essential addition to the AMHF Books program. *Personality: How It Forms* is jargon-free, and as such is intended for general readers as well as professionals. Dr. Kellerman probes the deep and eternal questions facing any practitioner: What is personality? What motivates the individual? How does anyone become, and come to understand, the person he or she is?

The costs of promoting research, preparing translations, organizing workshops, and disseminating the findings of AMHF and AMHF Books are high. For this reason, all sales of AMHF Books as well as donations of any amount on the Web site via PayPal, constitute a meaningful contribution to the public good. We thank you for helping us improve the lives of our citizens and building a more compassionate society.

americanmentalhealthfoundation.org

Introduction

Are you born that way (genetically), or did your personality just merely happen on its own—perhaps bit by bit as you got older and maybe in a kind of random fashion? Or, do you think your personality is written in the stars based upon your birth date? Or, are you reincarnated, and thus your personality comes from another time? Finally, do you believe your personality only formed throughout your childhood because of your experiences as you matured?

If your personality formed solely because of the experiences you had growing up, then perhaps genetics would have played a very little or no part at all in its formation. On the other hand, is it possible that everything about your personality is genetic and none of it is based on your experiences with parents and siblings, teachers, and friends?

Well, the answer is most likely that both genetics and experience in early childhood, in early family life, played an important role, now, in who you are. All of it together comprises the basic seeds that eventually accounted for the growth and appearance of one's full personality.

Is It Biology Over Culture or Culture Over Biology?

The answer to the question of how your personality became what it is—how it formed—actually concerns a commonsense understanding. Therefore, what most likely occurred is that we are all born with certain genetic dispositions or inclinations to be, or behave in, a certain way, and also, that for sure, as we continued to develop and mature, our experiences figured into the formation of our personality in a highly significant way. So that both are true: we are genetically (but probably in a general sense) disposed to be a certain way, and along with this our experiences during childhood and thereafter played at least an equal, if not even more important, part in the formation of the personality with which we wound up.

The question about which is the greater influence on personality—culture (our experiences), or biology (our genes), may really be a question of whether it's even possible for one to triumph over the other. That is to say, in the formation or development of personality, is biology (genetics) triumphant (Does it win?), or is it possible that culture can triumph over biology (Is it that our experiences are dominant)? Is it that environmental, social, and cultural influences can mold biological givens, or are we robots that only play out the instructions of our genes so that almost most of the time, or even all of the time, we are not really thinking and feeling people who can make choices not originally programmed in our genes?

The answer in this book is that Yes, we are born with a genetic program, and that Yes, our brains are wired a certain way, and Yes we do have instincts. However, in addition (and it is a big addition), we are all also very much sculpted by our experiences, by contact with significant people in our lives, and that we are especially influenced through the demands that society places on us through interaction with family, peers, school, work, and play, and in terms of the overall effect of our successes and failures—and of course, and very specifically, on how we were cared for, growing up.

Because of this significant cultural, environmental (non-biological) influence, it becomes quite possible to trace or map these specific influences that can, and frequently do, make us or break us. And it is such experiences that can have the greatest impact in the formation of personality—perhaps, but only "perhaps," a victory for culture.

"The Flesh on the Bones"

With respect to genetics, we know that each person's overall mood—whether energetic or not, whether up or down, whether inhibited or not, and so forth—is frequently spotted by family members early on in one's life. We hear people say, "He was always very active—never really wanted to take naps;" or, "She never smiled much, and was always shy;" or, "Even from the beginning, he never would look you straight in the eye." And generally speaking, we ourselves know that parts of our own behavior as well as a fair variety of our preferences have not really changed that much throughout our lives. Certainly, our tastes, sensibilities, talents, and intellect emerged more gradually, but all of it was for all intents and purposes, "the flesh on the bones," the kind of socialization we developed that surrounded our core genetic dispositional mood, or basic genetic form with which we all nakedly arrived in this world.

A good example might be the person who always—even from the beginning—showed a kind of withdrawn moodiness, and who then developed personality traits to accommodate this core, basic and central psycho/genetic orientation. An illustration of personality development including emotions and personality traits that surround and support such a central in-born orientation of withdrawn moodiness may include an assemblage of inclinations such as shyness, cynicism, pessimism, and possibly even argumentativeness, sullenness, and hostility. In other words someone who is born with a kind of withdrawn tendency will have a higher than average probability to also likely develop such a cluster of personality traits and emotions connected to the withdrawn tendency that includes the correlated inclinations of shyness, cynicism, pessimism, argumentativeness, sullenness, and even perhaps hostility.

In contrast, a person who is born with a smiling and friendly tendency toward others will most likely develop characteristic emotions and personality traits that include: inclinations to express friendliness, sociability, optimism, cooperativeness, and an overall agreeableness.

Now, here comes the influence of culture; that is, even when someone is born with an inclination toward the inhibition of expressiveness, or even a noticeable shyness, a very understanding and emotionally giving environment can definitely make a difference in minimizing the genetic tendency toward such inhibition and avoidance of spontaneity, and in contrast, maximize an accumulation of better sociability and greater emotional expressiveness.

We do have anecdotal evidence that the power of culture generally, and more specifically the nature of family influence—how you're brought up—will most likely carry the day, or at least make a big difference to how you eventually will turn out. This means that environmental influences are tremendously important in how one's personality will eventually look. And such influences include that of family, peers, teachers, and also frequently includes others you may idolize as you're in the process of finding figures with whom to identify so that you too, can be like them.

This sort of cultural influence on genetic endowment is referred to in the scientific literature as *epigenesis*. It means that environmental influences can either trigger or inhibit genetic givens or potentials.

The main point is that personality traits are hugely influenced and developed through experience, but the experience that resonates, or rings a bell for any person will be that which better corresponds to the person's, shall we say, greatest in-born emotional propensity, or mood. On the other hand, when one's environment values a set of behaviors and sensibilities that are in contrast with the so-called in-born mood (positive or negative), and then such environmental influence succeeds in minimizing the respective mood by reinforcing and fortifying an opposite tendency, then such a scenario is an even more almost perfect example of the rather important phenomenon of the selective triumph of culture over biology.

Thus, even at an early point in life, environment can at the very least somewhat change, alter, modify, or slightly massage one's basic emotional tendencies, and at the very most, even drastically change basic emotional tendencies or mood dispositions to the extent that such a change would definitely qualify as a bona fide emotional transformation of basic personality type or style.

In this sense, the genetic program that we all show at birth can be defined as our basic personality dispositional silhouette or skeleton, and the environmental experiences that then consistently and relentlessly influence us comprise the make-up, the complexion of personality traits we acquire throughout our growing-up years. It is such a make-up of our developing personality that constitutes the so-called meat, or flesh on the bones.

The issue here is the flexibility of the system of personality; that is, even though the genetics of a person determines initial mood, nevertheless the influence of a person's experience can take that overall mood and shape it into a more specific enhancement of traits of the personality, or on the down side, a more specific derogation of the personality. The in-born mood therefore, can actually get better or worse—respectively, either can be elevated or degraded by healthy or by unhealthy early experiences.

Is There Such a Thing As an "Evil Gene"?

One of the conclusions here is that the idea or belief that someone can be born specifically evil (and not just with an overall general negative mood), doesn't make the grade. Specific evil in behavior is a function of experience.

You are not born with an evil gene!

You have to learn to be bad, or even, left to one's own devices, in the absence of decent parenting (or even partial or begrudging parenting), a child will usually recede to the lowest common denominator and be subject to all sorts of nefarious influences. And then ultimately, in such a non-nurturing, non-learning, and even pernicious environment, a person can develop emotions and personality traits with a high probability-prediction that such a person will consistently engage in acting-out behaviors covering the range from consistently getting into minor scrapes, to lying and stealing and breaking the law, to violating others, to overall serious delinquent behavior, and in extreme cases, even to the point of committing capital crimes.

Thus, growing up in a non-nurturing and non-learning environment leaves one to the fate of instinct and impulse, and then bad things can and do happen. And this was not a function of genes. There is no program in the genes to do evil. Rather, it's in the nature of early in-life particular negative experiences that make the difference for any person. Therefore in considering the issue of a possible gene that carries evil—forget it!

Every analysis tells us that culture or environmental influences have tremendous power in the development of personality, perhaps, and very likely, even more so than genetic givens. Yet, despite the optimism of such a finding, the idea of such powerful environmental influences also has a downside. And this leads us to a discussion of the influence of peer relationships and its power of persuasion on the developing personality. The question becomes: Which is more persuasive with respect to the developing personality, peer pressure or the influence of the family? And the answer really follows a simple formula—to wit:

1. If the family strives to counteract popular culture, then family influence will prevail over peer pressure;

2. If the family does not strive to counteract popular culture, but instead supports popular culture (even embracing it), then peer pressure will far outweigh family influence.

The Importance of Inner Controls

In the sense of healthy development then, the best head-start program is the family. It's in the family that we learn the importance of controlling impulses, where we then "internalize," actually infuse (take in) and develop controls, so that eventually we don't need anyone to tell us how to behave in a civilized manner, and where we then show that we can and do control our impulses, and that we can eventually do it ourselves without permanent adult supervision. We can become autonomous—be civil on our own so that no one will have to tell us what is right or wrong. We will know it on our own.

Therefore, the argument over whether an evil gene exists dissolves in the face of the profound importance of environmental influences on emotions and personality. In addition, to use an analogy, we also can see that our genes provide us with the tools to build the house, but again, it is the experiences we have with our environment that will eventually determine the kind of house we build with those tools, how we'll use those tools to build the house, and, eventually how the house looks, and finally how satisfied we are to live in that house.

In a sense, it all boils down to whether that house is constructed in a way that enables one to absorb tensions and anxieties, and difficult times generally, without the walls falling in and the house crumbling. In other words, if environmental influences and experiences with life and early family living were good and healthy, then one develops personality that has great resilience. And with respect to such resilience—the ability to withstand pressures of all sorts and not fall apart—a person is then able to correctly balance how to manage impulses within the personality with the necessary controls one would have normally internalized which then can triumph over impulses.

And to have sufficient controls to be able to control impulse is crucial for successful living. Therefore, with the ability to calibrate impulses in a healthy manner, one is tuned into life in a way that makes functioning easier. Because of such good tuning in, one can better integrate the demands that continuously and even relentlessly come to us from the environment. And the successful ability to handle such adaptable integration of environmental demands is proof-positive of the value of decent early experiences that enables the personality to gestate good shock-absorbers—defined usually as resilience.

And here's the even better news. The importance of the internalizing of controls based upon early nurturing regarding how to wait (to have patience), and how to not always insist on moment to moment gratification, and most importantly to have valuable activity in your life that arrests and absorbs your attention and then of course gives you a sense of achievement, is the most valuable thing of all. It will enable you to have an important primary relationship, raise a family, earn a living, and achieve any number of important things—important goals.

But here's the rub! What if one has not successfully internalized controls? In such a case, the absence of a good balance of forces in the personality (better controls over impulses) places the person in a position to be inclined to generate acting-out behavior; that is, behavior that will get the person into trouble based upon an unbridled and decisively dyscontrolled pattern of impulsive behavior.

And this idea of the importance of "the balance of forces" in the personality leads us to understand the aim of this book.

The Aim of this Book

In this book, we will try to understand how impulses and controls work, how personality traits develop with respect to the issue of impulses and controls, how the emotions are connected to personality traits, and then specifically, how personality forms. We will see what it is that forms the muscle, the substance (personality attributes) on the basic structure (the skeleton or genetic endowment) of the personality. It is this frame of personality onto which everything about our personality adheres. It's about how culture "clothes" wear on genetic givens.

The question is: What are the elements of personality that adhere or stick to this frame? The answer is that the mechanisms that help keep that frame or skeleton of personality hard, resistant to change, and consistent, so that everyone agrees that who you are is really who you are, consists of a variety of elements that are connected to the overall personality. These agglomeration of elements comprise the identifiable "you"—the emotional/psychological skin and muscle that adheres to, or covers the personality—that covers its blueprint, frame or skeleton. This identifiable "you" includes typical emotional expressiveness, mood, style of thinking, profile of personality traits, the balance of impulses and controls of the personality, the mechanisms of defense that aid in the management of anxiety, the system of emotion, and the multitude of factors that comprise all the aspects of the personality.

And this is precisely what we are about to do in this book. We will map the ins and outs of personality so that you will see how your personality formed. And we will present this material element by element so that the formation and specific picture of your personality and how it began to build and gain traction as something absolutely identifiable about you can be seen in a straightforward manner. And all of these phenomena—this magical kaleidoscope of the mind (the psyche)—will be put together displaying how these facets of personality came to connect and to ultimately crystallize the personality.

The promise of this book about how your personality forms will be made clear when all of these elements of personality, like a puzzle, are joined. Then a clear picture will be developed so that in turn you may be able to see a faithful reflection of how your own personality formed.

The Format of this Book, Part 1

In part 1 of this presentation, we will examine how the personality is wired—that is to say, what are the elements surrounding the supportive structure or skeleton of the personality—of what is it composed, and what do we call it? *Part 1* is entitled *The Wiring of the Personality* and will contain an analysis of the various facets of the personality. These facets or aspects of the personality include: the nature of one's wishes; the appearance of psychological/emotional symptoms; how memory plays a part in personality development; an analysis of the anatomy of acting-out and its significance with respect to various issues of personality development; an analysis of the crucial issue of the relation of impulses to controls; as well as an analysis and definition of what is meant by defense mechanisms of the personality. In addition, how anxiety figures in all of it will be discussed in terms of the operation of anxiety and its basic function in the personality, as well as the variety of effects anxiety has on the personality. And of course in the process of development, identification with significant others becomes essential.

How it all works will include a rendition of how to understand it all—of everything that motivates the personality including why we all behave the way we do. This means that we will ask the question as to what it is that we all needed to deal with in our lives that ultimately got the personality a jump start—even from the beginning of life.

We will look at the issue of memory, and conclude with the one dynamic interplay in the personality that if followed—like following a trail—will lead us to understand the entire interaction of the wiring of the personality with relation to how it all works.

The one thing to remember is that Yes, personality is consistent, and predictable, and that each of us has a personality signature that is composed of a basic spine or so-to-speak, a chassis (meaning a basic configuration or skeleton) that in turn is adorned by emotions, personality traits, impulses and controls, the operation of anxiety, a wish-system, a system of defenses, and the mechanics in the psyche (the mind) that enables psychological/emotional symptoms to exist—and yet, happily, at the same time this personality system has the ability (and the capacity) to adapt in order to enable an ironing out of wrinkles and a working out of problems of the personality.

Therefore, in part 1 all of these issues will be considered so that the reader will be able to appreciate how the personality begins to cohere around specific themes that in turn reveal the knitting together of these various facets of the personality.

The Format of this Book, Part 2

Part 2 of this book, *The Basic Personality Styles*, contains twelve chapters preceded by *Previews*. These *Previews* will simply list and briefly define 12 basic personality types or styles.

The twelve basic styles are divided into four categories. These four categories are all defined by how the person manages the pressure and challenge of emotions and therefore how we manage this challenge of emotions will give us a bird's eye view into how good we are in balancing the controls we have over the impulses we have.

For example, the first category is labeled *Emotion-controlled Styles*. This category contains personality styles that are governed essentially by the person's need to control emotion. A second category is labeled, *Emotion-dyscontrolled Styles,* and reflects the person's need to avoid the control of emotion; that is, this style of personality needs to express emotion, to yield to its release. A third category is identified as containing *Emotion-attached Styles,* in which the particular personality style is basically a dependent/ attached one so that the person's main objective is to be able to have someone on whom to depend. The final category is labeled, *Emotion-detached Styles,* and lists those types that are particularly allergic to the intensity of emotion, and who also avoid attachment—they feel that being with people creates a need to respond emotionally which is what they really don't want to do.

Each of the twelve basic personality styles or types reflects a person's personality signature—a signature that also can be seen as the consistency of that personality—its settled hard core around which is contained all the other facets of the personality.

In addition, analyses and descriptions of each of the twelve personality styles will also contain an end part in which will be presented the benign form of that particular style (described as "The More Normally Inclined Style") so that the reader may have an additional opportunity to identify and see the difference between each classic personality style as well as the less intense and more normally inclined view of that style. Therefore, by following the chapters carefully, one will be better able to understand one's own personality formation and see where you might recognize those parts of such personality styles that seem familiar.

The final chapter of the book will list a number of diagnoses or other mixed personality styles that have played a role in forming the history of how people have been diagnosed and described, as well as clarifying what is really meant by the popular phrase: nervous breakdown.

PART ONE

The Wiring of the Personality

Introduction to Parts 1 and 2 of this Book

The Frame or Skeleton of Personality and the Form of Basic Personality Styles

The wiring of personality is much the same as the wiring of the brain. The phrase we all hear from others, and also use ourselves, is: "The brain is wired that way!" This means that there are certain things we do because as a result of the way our species is—the way we are—we just do them automatically, as though these behaviors or attitudes were not ever the result of learning. So it's true, that even with respect to personality, when anyone's personality gets "fixed," it is almost as if the contours, texture, and basic nature of such a personality type is cast, as it were, in a permanent way, and therefore the configurations of personality are not subject to very much change. It is pretty much what we are.

Yet, we also know that we can be different in personality (how we respond whenever we find ourselves in varieties of situations and conditions, and also depending on who are our companions at the time). So that yes, personality is quite consistent although we can utilize what we know to adapt our behavior to just about, or almost whatever the situation calls for. It does not mean that we are all split personalities. What it does mean is that personality is flexible so that, whoever we are, we can temporarily shape how we respond (our personality) in ways that make us feel more comfortable. How we choose to do that is based upon whether we view the environmental condition in which we find ourselves to be friendly, familiar, and accepting, or unfriendly, strange or in some way threatening.

Nevertheless, over time, people who know us will understand who we are in the sense that our responses to things can be predicted. In addition, such prediction is based upon how people get to see our personality traits—these traits and their emotional underpinnings that are really consistent over time—even though we are able to calibrate how we behave (calibrate such traits) based upon all sorts of conditions that impinge upon us.

Of course, because of modern-day therapies even fixed traits can be massaged or changed. Such change starts from the fixed position of who we are—in a position that is identifiable to anyone who knows us—as being us. And it is only from such a consistent position of who we are that the changes that take place emerge or occur in relation to who we were. And based upon who we were enables us (anyone) to see the difference in who we have become. In any event, any change that takes place in the personality certainly requires a shift in how we are affected by our anxieties and emotions and how we manage these anxieties and emotions.

At last, and during our post-adolescent years—when the personality, having matured and assimilated significant changes in style as well as substance, and when therefore the personality is more or less complete—a small number of basic personality styles or types can be identified and then actually can be classified. But even with respect to such basic elemental categories, most people reflect parts and various intensities of personality traits drawn from several of these basic categories.

As cited in the introduction, these categories are few in number, and can be enumerated as follows.

Basic Personality Styles

Category 1
Emotion-controlled Styles
These are personality styles that display the person's value and attitude in *controlling emotion*. In this sense, the person values strict

control over emotion so that this control of emotion is the real motive—the essence—around which the personality traits of each particular emotion-controlled style has cohered. These are the emotion-controlled styles or personality types of the obsessive-compulsive, the paranoid, and the so-called schizoid styles.

The Obsessive-compulsive Style—Basically defined as a person who is concerned with orderliness, and with rules and regulations. In a more vivid description, such a person is perfectionistic, overly conscientious, usually rigid and stubborn, and likes *to control* everything. It is what counts as *emotional control.* Such persons are frequently repetitively fixed on thinking about something, and this is what is referred to as "obsessive" and ruminative. The reference to "compulsive" refers to the impelling need to do the something that was obsessed about. Thus, the obsessiveness is the thinking, and the compulsiveness, the doing.

The Paranoid Style—Distrust and suspiciousness characterize this type of person. Yet, the basic characteristic that essentially is the core quality that informs this type is the tendency toward being *critical.* This is the kind of person who criticizes everything unfamiliar, and will find it extremely difficult to permit anything "in"; that is, such a person will not be easily able to do new things, or make new relationships, or even to change one's routine. Thus, the prime effect and motive of this person's criticality is to guard or *control* emotion. Therefore, *guardedness, guardedness, guardedness* is the psychological mantra here—essentially meaning that the person is especially and inappropriately concerned with "letting-in" anything new.

The Schizoid Style – The way such a person realizes the need *to control* emotion, is by way of restricting emotional expression. Thus, such a person shows a flat emotional response and is usually involved in activities that do not require very much social interaction. Even though this person is also emotionally detached, nevertheless, the aim of controlling emotion by flattening it makes such an individual quite representative of the emotion-controlled type. A quality of social *remoteness* is central here. The personality characteristic of "reserved" is the least-onerous quality of such a remote personality style, whereas "withdrawn," or "detached," or "aloof" reflect a more socially morbid cast to the personality.

Category 2
Emotion-dyscontrolled Styles
These are personality styles that display the person's value and attitude in keeping emotion *from* being controlled. It is a style that is quite opposite from the emotion-controlled style. This kind of person's aim is to keep emotion in a dyscontrolled state—in a state wherein *emotion triumphs over control*, and therefore persons with such styles are also characterized by a rather continuous tendency to be attracted by, and to create situations in the environment that generate endless stimulation and excitement. In this way boredom and stillness, which would create anxiety for such a person, are avoided. These are the emotionally dyscontrolled styles (or personality types) of the "histrionic," "narcissistic," and "psychopathic" styles.

The Histrionic Style – In this behavioral disposition a need for attention dominates the person's life. This kind of person needs to be central, usually dramatic, and also seeks circumstances in which the motive to be seductive can be displayed. At the core of the personality however, is a very high *suggestibility*. This is the kind of personality type that can be easily hypnotized, and who also can predictably easily fall in love. Because of such "suggestibility" traits, this histrionic (or hysterical) personality needs to deny any information that contradicts the person's yearnings, insofar as this denial mechanism in the personality contains a typical strategy that invites-in or selects-in what the person wants; and simultaneously screens out any information that would contradict or show that what the person wants or yearns for is not good.

The Narcissistic Style – The narcissist demands attention and *adoration*. It is a personality style that assumes *entitlement*, and can show a failure of judgment in the sense of overreacting when entitlements are withheld. Because of such an over-entitled state of mind, this failure of judgment can be quite troubling and can create endless difficulty for such a person—due to the probability of the creation of untoward events that will likely occur due to such poor judgment. Along with this, such a person will usually become exploitative when circumstances seem right for having an advantage. This person also can be arrogant, and frequently shows an absence of sufficient empathy especially when the person's primary goal of having the freedom to express emotion can be assured. This narcissistic person focuses all interest on the self. Nothing seems more important to this sort of narcissistic need than gaining adoration and advantage.

The Psychopathic Style – This kind of person is also referred to as an *Antisocial Personality*. The behavioral style seen here reflects a clear *absence of respect for boundaries*. This lack of concern about the boundary between self and others results in delinquent behavior as indicated by the wide variety of acts of disregard for others as well as overall acting-out behavior. Such a person is profoundly irresponsible, lies, cheats, and otherwise is preoccupied with manipulative acts that also assure the unrelenting release of emotion. In addition, such a person needs to create endless stimulation as a way of not being *still*. Presumably, being *still* is terribly worrisome for such a person because it is theoretically assumed that the person's inner life is bereft of any extensive richness of thought. The only cognition (thought) occupying such a person concerns how to have advantage and gain the ascendancy in any self-aggrandized way that can offer gratification with respect to taking short-cuts and getting what is wished.

Category 3
Emotion Attached Styles (Dependent)

These are individuals who continue to be highly influenced by parents or others in authority positions. In this way, tension regarding emotions is managed by the *sense of attachment* and therefore, such individuals gain a sense of security through affiliation with the figures on whom they depend. In this sense, disagreements and anger are limited, and decision-making that could possibly count as independent thinking is similarly avoided. These are the emotionally attached styles or personality types of the "dependent," "passive-aggressive," and "inadequate" styles.

The Dependent Style – In this style of relating, *remaining attached* to the caregiver is the desired way of managing the challenges of life. With the assurance of such attachment, the dependent person is not overly worried about being overwhelmed by emotion. And this is important for such a person because to be overwhelmed by emotion is equivalent to a condition in which there is an absence of someone on whom to rely. In terms of reliance on another, rather than implementing activity toward goals, such a person usually depends on magical wishes to feel gratified. And in this way, such a person equates *wishing* with *doing*, and the gratification of achievement is then frequently experienced through the wishing. All of this suggests a need to be cared for that generates a rather high-level sensitivity to anything resembling separation from the caregiver. It is the kind of personality style that shows submissive behavior, as is usually the case in people who have difficulty in disagreeing with others as a way of basically ensuring the best possible relationship with another person on whom to depend.

The Passive-aggressive Style – This person retains the need for attachment to the parental figure or other authority, but is usually engaged in a *power struggle* implying a protest, and even anger, over such dependency, or need for attachment. The manner of managing emotion (specifically the emotion of anger) occurs in one of three ways: as in a *passive stance;* as in an *aggressive stance;* or, as in a strictly *dependent stance.* In the *passive stance,* anger is expressed through delay; that is, the person expresses hostility through a delay of response. In the *aggressive stance,* anger is expressed with a subtle preemption—that is, with a touch of arrogance. In the *dependent stance,* anger is expressed through an excessive cloying or annoying dependency. The basic strategy of the passive-aggressive person is the automatic unconscious design of behavior that enables the person to express hostility and importantly, to have the other person feel it, and yet, because of the seeming innocence of the passive-aggressive person, attachment to others can be usually sustained on the basis that such passive-aggressive responses were ostensibly not deliberate nor meant to be hurtful.

The Inadequate Style – This person is entirely wishful for full support from the authority figure—usually the parent. It is the kind of person who manages emotion by just about fully *under-responding.* Such under-response is even to simple everyday challenges that people face—typically represented in all arenas of the person's life. Therefore, such a person requires consistent support from the caregiver or helper. The under-response is a way to limit expression of any decisive emotional reaction, and in the absence of more decisive emotional expression, the person experiences greater safety. The idea of safety is central in this person's life. Performance of jobs that such a person may undertake, or requirements given to such a person render the performance almost always below average, or the fulfillment of requirements invariably predicate an anticipated failure.

Category 4
Emotion Detached Styles (Sensitive/Vulnerable/Withdrawn)

These are persons who manage emotion by *keeping away from entanglements with others,* or who exhibit erratic behavior when feeling too close to others. In order to avoid anxiety, such individuals seem overly sensitive in social situations in which insecurities can feel as though they could possibly or actually fragment the personality. Ultimate social isolation is the effect of such styles. The fear of emotional closeness is minimized because of the isolation, so that the person is able to feel more secure. These are the emotionally detached styles or personality types of "borderline," "depressed," and "avoidant" styles.

The Borderline Style – This person manages tension and emotion by limiting relationships. Any sense of closeness is contaminated by erratic and/or explosive reactions. The *instability of relationships* is characterized by impulsivity, recklessness, and irritability. The irritability is connected to a particularly strong sensitivity to relationship events; that is, the borderline-personality individual finds it almost impossible to tolerate any sustained relationship without having angry and sudden outbursts of temper. It is what is known as *a thin stimulus barrier;* that is, reacting with an over-sensitivity to anything that is even slightly unsettling.

The Depressed Style – This is a person who has had a *long-standing but not psychotic depressive mood.* A deflated sense of self-esteem is typical here, and the person can be very insecure, self-absorbed, and self-protective. Such a person may over-identify with objects of pity as in the example of feeling heartbreak over a wounded animal, but in any personal relationship an absence of demonstrative affection toward the partner is evident, and even though such a person may perceive the self as generous and considerate of others, the net effect of the depressive-personality dynamic is that such a person is almost entirely absorbed with personal tensions and not in any authentic way really concerned about the needs of others. When pointed out, however, and in particular situations, surprisingly, such a person can adjust and be quite caring of the other. This sudden change of attitude is usually a function of sensitivity to possible rejection.

The Avoidant Style – This person manages emotion by becoming *socially inhibited*. Such avoidant behavior is usually due to excessive feelings of inadequacy—in popular culture referred to as *an inferiority complex*. An intense fear of potential criticism from others is also a frequent concern of such a person. As a result of this sort of social tension, the person is especially risk-averse, and is preoccupied in the endless search for self-assurance. Because of such habitual avoidance behavior, this person begins to lack sufficient and significant exposure to normal everyday social experiences so that when actually presented with the opportunity to participate in a social circumstance, the event will seem awkward and the person will generally feel frightened or irritable, and either will want to avoid such a situation, or immediately depart if actually co-opted into such a circumstance.

Summary

These personality styles largely represent a complement of basic types that develop specific ways to manage the operation and expression of emotion. The styles are developed either *to control* emotion, or to be sure not to control it (to have emotion be *dyscontrolled*), or to remain emotionally *attached* (as in being dependent), or to remain emotionally *detached* (as in being separate—sensitive, vulnerable, withdrawn).

The styles click into place rather early in development and constitute what can be considered to be a hard-wiring of the personality. Once the style crystallizes, it becomes etched, so that the style, or type, is singularly identifiable, resistant to change, and becomes the so-called basic frame, or structure, (or skeleton) of the personality—its characteristic way around which will form all other facets of the personality.

These twelve basic styles will be spelled out in greater detail in part 2, chapters 6 to 17, so that the essential color of each personality can be better observed. The basic styles will be presented in terms of how each one manages the challenge of emotion, as in *emotion-controlled styles, emotion-dyscontrolled styles, emotion-attached styles,* and *emotion-detached styles.*

It also needs to be noted that these are personality styles defined as psychiatric states meaning that the focus is on understanding how tension and anxiety is managed. And when seen through such a psychiatric lens, it becomes apparent that what is revealed concerns the issues that are so-called wrong with the person. Because of this psychiatric bias regarding personality formation and its developmental effects, in part 2 explanations of each personality style will be presented that describe how such a person can be identified with a psychiatric diagnosis yet reflect behavior that is more normally inclined despite the particular psychiatric underpinning of such a personality identification; that is, essentially showing a more normally inclined person even though the diagnosis remains a psychiatric one.

But at this stage, we will begin with the *Wiring of the Personality* that includes the importance in personality development of issues of: memory as in *remembering*, the influence of a person's *wishes* and how these are related to the appearance of *symptoms*, the reason for the appearance of *acting-out* behavior, the existence in the personality of *impulses* and the importance of the relation of impulses to mechanisms of *controls*, and finally, to an examination of the operation and function of *defense mechanisms* in the personality.

Therefore, we will examine what surrounds and accounts for the particular form, or wiring of the personality, by looking at, and examining the issues of:

1. Remembering—in contrast to repression of memory wherein the individual suppresses the memory of significant events and/or experiences;

2. Wishes—the effect on the personality of wishes that are achieved versus those that are thwarted;

3. Symptoms—the appearance of emotional/psychological symptoms in the personality and how and why they occur;

4. Acting-out—why a person "does" something (as in acting-out), rather than "know" something (as in not acting-out) is a telling factor in the operation of the personality;

5. Impulses—what they are and what they do;

6. Controls—the importance of controls and their relation to impulses;

7. The Maturation Ratio between controls and impulses;

8. Defense mechanisms—their design for the management of emotion;

9. Defense mechanisms—their design in the management of personality traits.

All of these particular benchmarks of personality development, when dissected and analyzed, reveal in great detail how the personality is put together displaying the entire wiring of the personality—the type of personality we have and its particular behavioral signature, it's style.

Then, in part 2, I present these basic personality types and styles along with actual clinical examples of each (and as mentioned above) also with reference to how each actual type may appear when expressing a more normally inclined personality style of that type.

CHAPTER ONE

Remembering

W<small>E CAN BEGIN</small> to enter our journey into the process of personality formation by examining the essence of what the psychoanalyst-as-therapist is looking for. If we boil it down to its essence, and try to use one word that characterizes this psychoanalytic undertaking of seeing how the personality is formed, that word would be, *remembering*.

Psychoanalysts want patients to remember. Obviously, this remembering refers to something related to one's past, to one's history, to one's childhood. When we remember what it is that we need to remember, we will then step onto the first level of the scaffold—the platform from which we will begin to understand what underpins all of personality formation. Access to this scaffolding will be the vantage point from which we will be able to see the entire superstructure on which personality rests—level by level.

The psychoanalyst starts you off by asking you to practice remembering. For example, at some point toward the beginning of the treatment, the analyst will probably ask you to report a dream. But when the patient indicates that he or she cannot remember dreams so well, so that to remember one he or she will need to write it down, in all likelihood the analyst will instruct the patient *not* to write it down. Rather, the analyst will encourage the patient to try *to remember* the dream in the absence of writing it, and in addition will instruct the patient to not report the dream to anyone else, because to repeat it will dilute the dream for the purpose of working on it and understanding it in the therapy session.

While waiting for the next psychotherapy session, the objective is for the patient to rehearse, recall, and recite the dream to him or herself for as many times as necessary to keep from forgetting it, and only then to describe the dream—and again, solely to the analyst. In addition, not reporting the dream to anyone else helps the patient "own" the dream and, finally, to work on it.

The purpose of this little instruction to the patient regarding the remembering of the dream is to encourage the patient to begin to struggle with *remembering* rather than to depend on a written log of the dream that basically excuses the patient from an active struggle to recall. In addition, this sort of struggle to keep trying to remember contributes to the patient's growth with respect to not being dependent on written material or other techniques of remembering that do not require such active struggle.

The point is that we all need to struggle—to pressure ourselves to think—and then to discuss what it is that comes to mind when trying to remember.

What Is It We Need to Remember?

Isn't it that each of us remembers different things, different experiences? Surely it can't be that we all do, in fact, remember the same thing. Or, another way of putting it is to consider that when we do finally remember, is it possible that it is the same thing that we all remember?

Is that what we're getting at when we are asked to remember our past—that we're all the same?

The fantastic answer is—Yes. *We all will remember the same thing!*

Again, What Is that Thing We Need to Remember?

What is it then that we need to remember? Another way to put it is to say that we need to be conscious of something. We need to be conscious of this something because as Sigmund Freud once said, "consciousness is curative." He meant that when something is out of your awareness, is repressed and out of your consciousness, this kind of forgetting is really a concealment—an unconscious concealment—of some important issue. And it's a concealment therefore that even you don't know about, despite the fact that it is you who is concealing it. And further, that the concealment creates problems and emotional and psychological symptoms; the good news is that to surface and uncover the secret, or what is hidden (even from the self), is possibly to cure the symptom. Therefore, Freud reasoned that surfacing the unconscious material that was pushed out of awareness, or repressed, would mean to remember it, and remembering it begins the process of cure.

So, presumably the important issue concerns what is concealed, unconscious, hidden, repressed, and therefore forgotten. To answer this question concerning what it is that is repressed and therefore forgotten (the things that we need to remember), first we ought to understand what it is that we are all required to do at the beginning of life when we start to talk and to hear from our elders what is permissible to do, and what the word *No* means. It is during this period of our development that the concealment and repression of what we need to now remember starts.

The Issue of Compliance

In reasonably normal family life wherein at least one parent is focused on the guidance of the child, the parent (or parents) are always (emphasis on "always") concerned about teaching and helping the child learn the do's and *don'ts* of civilized living. Of course, it's *the don'ts* that really count. "No, don't do that." And, "No, don't touch that." And, "No, you can't put that in your mouth." And, "No, you can't have that."And, "No, don't touch the stove, it's hot."

We all learn through the No's we hear. However, for infants and young children, hearing the No is always accompanied by an implicit "or else!" Even when the No's are uttered in pearly tones, all infants and children implicitly hear the "or else."And in fact, in many families, the "or else" is actually stated (and even perhaps threatened).

It is this implicit "or else," and how the child feels about it that gives us our first clue/glimpse as to what the child conceals even from him or herself. And it is the "or else," (whether actually implicit or not) that constitutes a threat. It is this implied threat that animates, encourages, and energizes the child's compliance. In addition, a child certainly also implicitly understands that the "or else" exists within the context of parental love and concern. Therefore, the child's compliance to parental instructions, values, and style, is the true engine that begins creating a sense of the reality of right and wrong, and actually a strong sense of "how to be." This "how to be" is, along with "the psychology of identification with significant others," the core to understanding personality development; in addition, another kind of compliance refers to the child's identification and internalization of the parents' attitudes and beliefs that become infused or blended into the entire formation of the child's personality. Furthermore, at the same time, however, something else gets created.

What Else Gets Created When the Child Needs to Comply?

We need to understand that all children, whether feeling loved or not, are always, and in some form, considering the possible idea of being abandoned. This is so because especially during early childhood, the thing that makes the child feel completely helpless is even the remotest thought of being without parental protection. This sense of helplessness (or disempowerment) is two-pronged. First is the sense of physical protection, and second is the sense of an even greater danger: emotional vulnerability that is really better understood as feeling an emotional terror. It is this apprehension, anticipation of possible abandonment along with accompanied assumed terror (of abandonment and vulnerability) that supports and wins the child's day in its incentive and willingness *to listen, to obey, to comply.*

Even though all of these factors (compliance, fear of abandonment, need for protection), are what influences the child, nevertheless, it doesn't matter how young one is, or how in need one is for protection; the fact is that for every person compliance is experienced as a form-of-force, or submissive acquiescence, or control, and will always because of this even vague sense of being controlled, generate anger, or even rage (conscious or not)—for the most part experienced implicitly, unconsciously. This is especially true for the young child who is at the mercy of the forces, and is not very well able to determine what is exactly happening—of being conceptually un-crystallized and therefore dependent for the most part on how things feel

Therefore, it seems that for this child such anger will also and always be generated to the condition of compliance. The main point is that every child will either always, or at some point, experience compliance as that of a forced compliance; and will reflexively be angry about it but usually not know about the anger in its fullest measure.

The question becomes, Why is this so?

The answer concerns what it feels like to have one's impulses, needs, or wishes, blocked—especially in a young child (or even, infant), who doesn't know much else except impulse, need, and wish. Basically, in a loving family it appears that the infant or young child gets, more or less, whatever it wants based upon parental attention and concern with the child's every whim and wish. But to this new being in the world, it surely does not feel as though each and every wish is met to the fullest measure exactly how it is needed and precisely when it is needed/wanted. Because of this condition of inevitable blocked wishes, the child experiences a profound pervasive sense of disempowerment or something that feels like that, seeming ubiquitous, permeating the child's sensations and emotions.

What Happens with this Anger?

Here the main point is that the child usually cannot show such anger (or even rage), because in the very young child the fantasy of abandonment—though imprecise, amorphous, or ambiguously felt/experienced as a general mood—then forces that anger to be concealed; that is, forces that dissatisfaction (the anger) to be repressed, and therefore hidden in the unconscious. In this way, since the anger is not expressed, or not expressed directly, nor not even conscious to the child, then in turn, the probability and also possibility of punishment, in the form of the parent abandoning the child, is just about zero. In other words the child automatically (and in a nanosecond) is able to conceal any anger; and so with no anger expressed or consciously experienced, there is no reason to be punished or more significantly, no reason to be abandoned.

Of course children do in fact show anger. But there is so much in the child's development and experience that urges or even demands compliance, that in the child's ongoing resistance to such demands, nevertheless, compliance-building does gradually take place and, correspondingly, anger does accompany it. But much of it is concealed by a process of repression, and hidden in the child's psyche—in his or her unconscious.

So what happens when the anger is so repressed? Primarily when the anger is repressed, the child really does not know of its existence. Rather, the child feels only that there is something vaguely wrong. In many cases, this feeling that there is something wrong usually transforms itself into the specific emotion of guilt. And to this emotion of guilt (about which the child knows no reason for such guilt even to exist), the child then wants to do good things so that the bad feeling of "the something-is-wrong" mood (the guilt) should be eliminated or erased. That is to say that when you do good things, then the guilt or feeling of "wrongness" is nullified, or should be nullified. When the guilt is erased, the child will feel good. And this feeling of feeling good means that ultimate and underlying endemic abandonment fears are brought to the zero position—also into repression.

Thus, we can see that even with a sort of incorrect sensation (the child's fear of abandonment) a decent outcome can be generated. Sometimes from a rather bad cause, paradoxically, a good result can occur. The child starts doing things the right way, and becomes a good citizen, largely out of a basic illusion, or even perhaps delusional fear—the fear of, and belief in, the possibility of abandonment, and therefore, a concurrent desire to be agreeable.

Again, What Is It that Needs to Be Remembered?

We can now see, that what needs to be remembered concerns in a plain and simple way, and perhaps in an unexpected way, an early sense of anger toward the parent that could not be directly expressed, or even was not itself accessible to the child's consciousness. Of course, many people cannot get to it—cannot put their finger on it; that is to say, can't *remember* it.

The question is: Can't remember what? What is the "it" that cannot be remembered? The answer is: The child cannot remember the sense of "the fear of abandonment" along with the subsequent compliance to rules and regulations, along with the repression of the anger about not getting the chance to satisfy whatever wish was involved to get whatever impulse needed to be expressed (or get whatever needs to be gratified) gratified. The good news is that it doesn't much matter if the person remembers it exactly because the same pattern begins to occur throughout childhood, and then, believe it or not, throughout life. This means what needs to be remembered or seen more clearly—consciously—is that people feel dissatisfied with others, or feel angry toward them, but for one reason or another are not able to express the anger directly, or even be conscious of the anger. This is what is meant about *the same pattern occurring throughout life.*

What needs to be remembered—where consciousness, as Freud says, can become curative—or what needs to be brought to consciousness, is a greater awareness of the fact that all of us are angry a lot of the time but do not really know it. We call it *being upset,* or *being bored,* or *feeling moody,* or *depressed,* or *dissatisfied,* or any number of other code words for feeling angry. And make no mistake about it, the anger is almost always about another person who prevented you from having something you wanted. And what the other person did to you is an essential thing to know about.

And this essential thing to know about is *always about the same thing.*

Isn't that strange? It is always, for all of us, about the same thing. And what is this thing that always will make us angry regarding what that other person did and on top of it, making it dangerous for us to express the anger directly?

That thing is the thwarting or blocking of our *wishes!* And this blocking of our wishes constitutes the moment of birth in the development of a psychological/emotional symptom. In fact, several principles are developed to indicate just how important such a process of blocked wishes and the reflexive response of anger is, to the development of a symptom—which also not only relates to the wiring of the personality but also demonstrates the effect of such wiring. These principles are:

Principle 1. Where there is a blocked wish, and if the anger to that blocked wish is repressed, not only will there be a symptom generated from such repression of the anger, but there must *be a symptom developed from such anger-repression.*

Principle 2. Where there is a symptom, not only will anger be repressed, but anger must *be repressed.*

Principle 3. Where there is no anger repressed, not only will there be no symptom, there cannot *be a symptom.*

Principle 4. Where there is no symptom, not only will there be no anger repressed, there cannot *be anger repressed.*

Yes, the blocking of a wish is the moment of the birth of a symptom. It is the conception of a symptom—like the moment of conception and is one example of the wiring of the personality and its effects. In this respect, in the following chapter the nature of wishes and symptoms is considered.

CHAPTER TWO

Wishes and Symptoms

WE ARE ALL wish-soaked creatures. What this means is that we are all governed by what is known as *the pleasure principle*. We all want what we want when we want it. And the wishes are the chief representative of the pleasure principle. This means that when we get our wishes met, we feel good and we feel empowered. However, when we don't get our wishes met, then we don't feel good, and correspondingly, we then feel disempowered.

The problem in all of this is that the world is constructed in such a way that there are too many variables—too many factors that affect everything we do—so that because of all these factors we rarely can control the situations in which we find ourselves. As a matter of fact, because of so many variables that impact us and our situations, we actually can never ever control it all. And therefore, because we cannot control everything in the way we would like, then most frequently, we don't get what we want. Even should we, indeed, get what we want, it usually is not exactly when we wanted it. And even if it should be exactly when we wanted it, frequently enough, it is not getting what we wanted to the fullest measure. And this is what we meant when describing how a young child (even an infant) might feel.

Because of this very incomplete gratification that we all experience, all of the time, we are therefore frequently either a little, or a lot frustrated. The point is that when wishes are not met, or even quite incompletely met, we will usually feel disappointed, dissatisfied, disgruntled, disgusted, or a combination of these *disses*. When the feeling or *dissatis-pointed-ness* sets in, it's a sure-fire bet that such dissatisfaction along with disappointment will generate feelings of annoyance, anger (even intense anger such as rage)— and in some, so-to-speak thin-egoed people, even fury.

Generally, or even usually, such disempowerment leading to angry feelings will be directed to another person because when wishes are not met or not gratified, it will most frequently be because someone is preventing the individual from getting what he or she wants—a job, a raise in salary, sex, approval, recognition, adoration, food, success, and so forth. It is what is referred to as *thwarted wishes*.

When this happens (the fact that someone is blocking you from getting what you want), your anger will most often not be able to be expressed toward the particular person frustrating you. This is so because it is likely that such a person either is a parent, boss, partner, teacher, client, customer, important friend, and so forth; at times, your anger toward such a person may be socially almost impossible to express. The conscious idea itself of this anger at that person can be automatically anticipated as a great threat to your security. In this sense of its seeming impossibility of expression, rather than knowing it (that you're angry), you will instantly, perhaps in a nanosecond—especially before you even know that the angry feeling exists toward this person—hide, conceal, repress this anger, and then bury it in your unconscious mind so that even you yourself will be practically, or in most likelihood absolutely, oblivious to its existence.

This happens a great deal of the time—to all of us. The question then becomes: *So what?* What really does it mean that we repress, or push down the anger?

When we push down the anger (repress it), it means that again, just like we did in childhood, we can't let the person know that we're angry. And the reason for this is that we automatically believe—we assume—that should the person know about our anger toward him or her, then he or she will do what? We then believe that they will reject us, fire us, hate us, leave us—*abandon* us. That's what it all boils down to. We repress anger because instead of confronting the issue—calling it abandonment—we now have more sophisticated code words for it: *rejected, fired, hated, left.* So just as we did when we where children, we are frequently afraid to be directly angry with those that hold our security in their hands, and this is reinforced by civilized standards of behavior—interestingly enough—by which we all live.

In this sense, in the formation of personality, the personality disruptions we develop (the emotional/psychological symptoms) are fundamentally based upon considerations of a deep structure in the operation of the person's psyche. The proposition about this state of affairs can be stated thus:

> *In the formation of personality the deep structure in one's psyche related to the appearance of psychological/emotional symptoms is composed of the relation of repressed anger regarding one's thwarted wishes toward an identifiable person.*

But such is what is underneath. That is usually the buried layer of personality. On top, however, is the emotion of caution (and even fear) about what could happen if those persons—the culprits who thwarted our wishes—knew we felt anger toward them. So, consciously, if someone tells us we are angry at so and so, we usually deny it simply because we may not know that we even harbor such feelings. On the other hand if we're told that we are fearful of that same person, we're usually more aware of the fear and can fairly quickly admit to and identify our apprehension or our fear. The code phrase for such apprehension or fear, is usually referred to as *respect for the other person.*

To Reiterate

Basically, what's underneath is concealed anger. What's on top is the rigmarole we do to create little scenarios based upon the strategies and tactics we concoct to help us get away from the fear of rejection or abandonment that we think could occur if the other person sees the anger that is beneath the social veneer. These little strategies and tactics turn out to be those consistent behavioral patterns of ours that help us massage situations in a way that others are sure not to see either the fear that is on top, nor the anger below—especially the anger that is below. As stated, most frequently we ourselves are not even aware of this anger below—we also do not see it.

It is these behavioral-personality patterns based upon needs to conceal underlying emotions (angers and dissatisfactions), that get displayed in ways that determine our social persona and that become etched in us, becoming recognizable as our signature-selves. When someone asks, "What's his personality profile?" they are really asking to see the configuration of these etched behavioral patterns so-to-speak—our personality signature: for example, whether we can be assertive to challenges confronting us, or whether we are passive or timid with respect to such challenges.

These personality or character (behavioral) patterns can be understood as the basic structure around which forms everything concerning the full nature of our personhood. No matter how we dress, how we feel, what we do, or even with respect to the symptoms we have, these all surround this basic frame or skeleton of personality that further is resistant as well to change, and that surprisingly (or perhaps not so surprisingly) some might even call a substance harder than steel. Yes, as a subject the character or personality structure may be among the hardest (impermeable as steel) and also a most intangible subject.

Intangible yet Hardest

We develop this pretty much hardened personality structure very early on so that even with age, or even advanced age, the so-to-speak chassis of personality (these behavioral patterns) are sustained, and can be plainly seen to exist. Even though such patterns are engraved, the personality is also in the adaptable sense plastic, so that we can become different in our personality expressions and demeanor based upon our needs, which get determined by particular social circumstances. This condition of the plasticity of personality, however, does not in any way nullify the basic structure of the permanent silhouette (skeleton) of individual personality. Plasticity of personality is consigned to the psyche. It is the psyche's way of utilizing defense mechanisms and social understanding to create the best adaptations to varieties of situations. Yet, the skeleton of the personality is composed of genetic givens plus all sorts of epigenetic factors (environmental circumstances and demands) that shape these genetic givens throughout the child's developmental stages.

When seeing the personality underpinnings this way, we are really looking at the wiring of the internal structure of the personality—ultimately guided and guarded by what's known as *the psyche,* loosely synonymous with "mind," analogous to how the pleasure principle (we're interested in everything pleasurable) is synonymous with wishes (wanting what we want, when we want it, and how we want it). We might even be able to say that the pleasure principle is to the wishes, as the psyche is to the mind, meaning as the wishes are the major representative of the pleasure principle, the mind is the most conspicuous representative of the psyche, and in fact, the mind represents the psyche.

The interesting and predictable thing is that wishes can get us in trouble.

How Do Wishes Get Us in Trouble?

It's really quite simple. Wishes can and do get us in trouble. The fact that we are all wish-soaked creatures, in itself, may not be a problem. The problem is that when the wish is blocked by someone, we get mad. Now, there's the problem.

Most people never make any distinction between major and minor wishes. Such people—all of us—treat each wish as though it were major. For example, not being able to find your wristwatch when you need it and when you know it is somewhere in the bedroom, becomes as frustrating and annoying, and can make you almost as upset, as when you know that you have actually lost it somewhere outside of the home.

Thus, again, people usually do not calibrate the difference between major and minor wishes, but treat them all as major. Further, people usually do not make any distinction between trouble and aggravation. Everything is treated as though it is trouble. And this is another form of not distinguishing between major and minor wishes.

In this sense, people are wound up most of the time, thinking about all the so-called and presumed major wishes that they've not gotten realized, as well as all "the trouble" they always have.

What Does this Have to Do with How Personality Forms?

What all of this means with respect to the formation of personality concerns the issue of a person feeling angry at not getting what he or she wants, how it is wanted, when it is wanted, and then, to the fullest measure. When you don't get what you want, when you want it, and how you want it, and to the fullest measure, then the wish is blocked, thwarted, and frustrated, and you also feel it just that way—you feel blocked, thwarted, and frustrated. Then as a reaction when the wish is so blocked, you will feel the absence of being empowered. In contrast, empowerment is always experienced when the wish is gratified. Rather, it is the feeling of helplessness or disempowerment that occurs when wishes are denied.

Pushing the Anger Down and Developing a Symptom

The psychology of the feeling of helplessness or disempowerment will usually lead to a person feeling angry and then frequently also to a repression or pushing of the anger down. Imagine how much anger is pushed down with respect to always, and automatically, defining any wish as a major one (rather than distinguishing major from minor wishes), and any inconvenience as trouble (instead of mere aggravation), and then feeling that you cannot get what you want—ever.

This means that for most of our lives, we are constantly trying to manage being angry, and that in so many cases, rather than know we are angry, we say we were upset, or that we are stressed (another code word for being angry), and then moreover, we repress or push the anger down. We push the anger down (suppress or repress it), because the people who thwart our wishes and thereby disempower us are usually those who for any number of reasons we dare not be angry with.

Then, what we get when we repress the anger is a symptom—an emotional/psychological symptom—and sometimes this perhaps can take the form of a physical symptom as well. For example, is it possible that hypertension or high-blood pressure could result from the impact of a continual repression of anger? The answer is maybe Yes, and maybe, No. If however the repression of anger is really a continuous pushing down of intense anger, like rage, and if this kind of condition continues over a long period of time, then yes, it is highly probable that hypertension along with any number of other physical symptoms could develop.

So the answer to the age-old question regarding the effect of emotion on physical conditions is a resounding *Yes.* Emotions can affect physical conditions, as well as produce symptoms of a psychological nature. And this includes conditions such as phobias, anxiety conditions, digestive disturbances, migraines, and so forth.

In the structure of personality, when the wish is blocked, when one cannot have what is wanted, one feels disempowered and anger is generated to this sense of helplessness or disempowerment. Apparently, what happens then is that in the unconscious mind (where repressed material resides), the wish is then transformed into a psychological/emotional symptom like a phobia, or anxiety reaction, or panic attack, or an intrusive thought (a thought you didn't necessarily want but becomes intrusive and you can't shake it), or an obsession (like repetitively thinking that you have not turned off the stove), or a compulsion (like needing to go to see if you have turned off the stove).

Once the symptom appears, no matter how much you can reason with it, the symptom always wins. Reason or reasonableness never cures a symptom. No matter how much logic is directed at the symptom, logic can never cure it. The symptom will not listen. In order to cure the symptom, we have to unravel it by beginning to know that we are angry at a particular person, and rather than having directed the anger to that person, instead we swallowed it, and therefore the anger directed itself at us.

This is the problem: that the anger is directed at the self.

The Personality of Anger

What if the anger is directed at the self? Well, the problem is that anger is a primary emotion, and all primary emotions like anger or fear, joy or sorrow, have basic personality inclinations. We can call these *tropisms*. For example, a general scientific illustration of this point can be explained by examining the phenomenon of phototropism as well as a hydrotropism. Phototropism will cause a plant to grow toward light, while a hydrotropistic plant will grow toward water. That is all *it* "knows." When something is tropistic, *it* only "knows" or has the impulse to do what defines the tropism.

The same is true of primary emotions such as anger or fear. For example, fear only *knows* to flee. Fear *wants* to flee. Disgust *knows* only to reject, or eject (vomit). Joy *knows* only to pulsate with happiness. And anger only *knows* to attack. Anger *wants* to attack. Thus, when anger is swallowed and directed at the self, it will attack the self since that is what it is supposed to do—that is what it's all about. It only *knows* to attack. Fear is all about fleeing, and anger is all about attacking.

Thus, primary emotions are governed only by their unidimensional nature and not at all in themselves, innately, influenced by civilization. Yet, of course, environmental influences do indeed have an impact on primary emotions but only insofar as such influence can redirect the aim of the emotion. But, the intrinsic nature of each primary emotion is that it is unidimensional (only has one instruction). Therefore, with respect to the emotion of anger, its personality only has one instruction: *Attack!* This unidimensional instruction in the very nature of anger figures hugely in the formation of an emotional/psychological symptom. For example, in the translation of the wish into the symptom, it is the anger that stokes the unconscious furnace in which this transformation of wish into symptom takes place. It is a metamorphosis like a caterpillar to cocoon to butterfly. Only in this case it is the wish alloyed into the symptom by the action of the repressed anger existing in the unconscious mind.

Said again: *It is the anger attacking the self.*

Therefore, the composition of the personality of anger acts upon the wish so that the wish is expressed as fully gratified, *but* in the form of a psychological/emotional symptom. It is a symptom understood as the metamorphosis of the thwarted wish combined with the repressed anger to yield this emotional/psychological symptom, and can be expressed as an equation: Thwarted wish + Repressed anger = Symptom.

The Personality Profile of Anger

If we analyze the personality of anger we will see that its attack proclivity can be spelled-out with respect to various facets of its attack nature.

- Anger has an aggressive drive. Like all primary emotions, it's inborn.
- Anger is expansive. It wants to get bigger.
- Anger has explosive potential. It wants to burst out.
- Anger has a confrontational inclination. It wants to get tough.
- Anger has an attack inclination. It wants to attack.
- Anger has an entitled frame of mind. It feels it has the right to get tough.
- Anger is an empowerment. It eliminates feelings of helplessness.

Knowing

Anger or any primary emotion *knows* what it's supposed to do—what it itself is all about. So that *knowing* seems to be a very special issue in the whole structure of personality. We know what we want, especially when we wish it.

Knowing is implicated in symptom development, in the expression of wishes, and very importantly in the unraveling of the symptom. For example, when we know that we need to try and focus on the possibility that we have repressed some anger, and further, realize that this anger was originally intended to be directed at a specific person, and even further, that we need to join the two (bring the anger to consciousness and identify *the who* toward whom the anger is intended), then this kind of knowing can actually and truly begin to defeat the symptom; that is, the symptom will no longer have a purpose as a symbol since the real problem (anger connected to the intended *who*—the person) is now made visible to the self (to us), and is now concrete and not some abstract oblique and opaque symbol (the symptom).

When knowing something is for whatever threatening reason not possible to us, we then do what is called *acting-out*. And this acting-out is just another form of a symptom. The acting-out can take innumerable forms. It can be seen in the form of stealing, being promiscuous, doing self-defeating things like being passive-aggressive (making others angry while not being obvious about the strategy you use that makes them angry, and not even knowing that you want to make them angry), and so forth.

If we follow the map of the acting-out, we can further unfold the personality, and so-to-speak, see it all laid out.

What We Have So Far in the Formation of Personality

We have the supportive framework or skeleton of the personality that is based upon:

1. The idea of early in-life *compliance* (common to all of us), that in turn
2. generates underlying *anger* (because of the necessity to restrain our impulses), which in turn
3. galvanizes a process resulting in a profile of *personality traits* that protect us—so that we can adjust and adapt.
4. This becomes our personality signature—*the skeleton of the personality* that everything else about personality, such as emotions, thinking style, needs, controls, impulses, attitudes, sexuality, and so forth adheres to, intersects, and interacts.
5. This personality profile of traits is generally called *character traits* – but not in the sense of ethics or morality. Rather, these are called character traits as in traits that are *characteristic* of the personality.

Furthermore, because of the pleasure principle that permeates everything about us, we turn out to be wish-soaked, and the proposition that hardly any wishes get realized at the moment we want them (or at all), in turn generates a process leading to the appearance of symptoms—meaning, psychological/emotional symptoms.

This process includes the reflexive reactions we have and their distortions:

6. that all wishes are major (even inconsequential ones); and
7. that all inconvenience (even the slightest), is trouble and not mere aggravation; and
8. in this sense, the blockage of major wishes (all wishes), and trouble (even though it is mostly, really only aggravation), leads to
9. anger (that is frequently repressed); and
10. this repression of anger will always produce -
11. emotional/psychological symptoms of the personality. Further, in order to unravel the symptom and, in addition see the facets of the personality laid out bare, it is valuable to examine
12. the nature of acting-out as it relates to the issue of "knowing" (having insight).

The repression of anger and the issue of acting-out lead us now to a further examination of the overall wiring of the personality and its effects.

The Wiring of the Personality

In this first section of the book regarding the wiring of the personality we have already examined the issue of what and why the personality forms: that is, on what basis does it become necessary to form the wiring of the personality—remembering, compliance, control of impulses, the anger about this control, the repression of the anger, and the importance of the reign of wishes that represent the pleasure principle and the effect of the thwarting of the wish in the development of symptoms and in acting-out.

In the following chapter, I examine the nature of acting-out and how this analysis can be the basis for understanding the entire wiring of the personality. Acting-out relates to how the personality permits impulse to reign supreme, as well as strongly implicating the operation of defense mechanisms. Furthermore, we will see that even though in reality a wish may be thwarted, nevertheless in the psyche (in one's mind) no wish will ever be denied; that is, the psyche insists that the wish be gratified in the form of a neurotic or perverse transmogrified product—as a symptom—an emotional/psychological symptom. Interestingly, in psychotherapy the only phenomenon (or thing) that can get cured is a psychological/emotional symptom—perhaps a phobia or an obsession, or an intrusive thought. All else in psychotherapy is an attempt to assist the patient in the ability to struggle better with life—with greater effectiveness and success. Life does not get cured. Only symptoms can be cured, nothing else.

Struggling better is the goal.

CHAPTER THREE

Acting-out

Acting-out is *doing* rather than *knowing*—nothing more, nothing less. What this means is that when a person continuously does something that is undermining to the self as well as to others (such as lying, stealing, showing a pattern of sexual promiscuity, and so forth), this sort of behavior reflects the triumph of impulses over the person's ability to use controls, as well as meaning that "the doing-act" is taking the place of "the knowing of something"—that is, that *the doing* is occurring rather than the person having insight about something regarding that selfsame person's feelings toward others—or, more specifically, toward another specific person. The point is that this definition of acting-out is one in which we can see and understand the beginnings of how the psyche uses defenses to prevent painful notions from being made conscious. In place of such knowing and insight, the psyche creates endless "doing" things that keep the subject in a steady state of external stimulation, essentially acting to prevent a knowing state of insight about the self.

The question of insight is highly important. Although insight cannot usually cure anything, nevertheless with insight one can then have direction to know how to get out of the woods. Of course the insight tells you which way is out and then you must start walking out in order to get out. You must *do* in order to have the insight to be effective. Therefore, "not knowing" keeps one in the woods without any direction for getting out. With respect to acting-out, "the not knowing" something is essential for it to take place. In a way, acting-out is like walking in circles with no direction whatsoever—with no insight.

As such, acting-out qualifies as a symptom. In fact the acting-out is the externalization of a wish. What this means is that in the formation of a symptom, the wish that you have gets transformed even transmogrified or transmuted into a symptom since *for sure,* you feel anger toward a particular person. That person will be the one who is preventing you from getting your wish gratified: it will be the one who thwarted the wish.

Whenever the case presents itself in a way that, for whatever reason, you cannot be direct with your anger, you may reflexively conceal that anger through repression. Then into the unconscious will go the anger that in turn acts to transform the wish that was thwarted into a disguised form. In disguised form, the wish appears in the form of a symptom like a compulsion or a phobia, or some acting-out symptom such as lying, or stealing, or any unlawful or delinquent behavior.

Thus in this case of the symptom of acting-out, whatever the delinquent act is, it always will be a disguised form of the wish. To understand the symptom is first to understand the wish as well as the anticipated tension surrounding it.

Tension

All of the acting-out variations, all of the wish-needs a person has, all of the repression that operates in the personality, all of the defense mechanisms of the personality (those defenses that manage transitory momentary emotional reactions as well as those that assure the development of attitudes) directly relate to the nature of tension.

With respect to the issue of tension and its effects, the pleasure principle of the personality (seeking complete pleasure as exemplified in the search for the gratification of any wish) seeks the elimination of tension—down to zero. This is what is meant by the Freudian idea that the pleasure principle is related to "the life-instinct," whereas the complete absence of tension can be related to a new understanding of "the death-instinct"—tension down to zero.

In the psyche, because of the pleasure principle, no wish will be denied, while in actual real events, wishes are denied quite frequently thereby subsequently corresponding to an increase in tension. Wish-gratified equals absence of tension in accordance with the pleasure principle as well as a corresponding sense of empowerment. Wish-denied, equals an increase of tension and a corresponding sense of disempowerment.

Therefore, in the psyche the aim is always to calibrate tension down, and this downward calibration of tension is always determined by the implicit directive of the pleasure principle. Therefore, in the expression of acting-out behavior (as is the case with many symptoms), tension recedes. For example, a symptom may also be defined as a result of an acting-in. It is the thwarted wish along with the anger-becoming-repressed (therefore directed at the self) that then is extruded or projected out, expostulated as it were, in an acting-out form. Therefore, in this acting-out form it could be said that the entire purpose of the acting-out behavior is to avoid tension; that is, because of the acting-out, the person doesn't *know* something that would increase tension (were it to be known), so that the acting-out (deleterious though it is), becomes a phenomenon causing immediate tension to recede. A good example of such an equation can be seen in the analysis of the symptom of self-mutilation behavior (as in cutting). The acting-out person (the cutter) always, without exception, reports a relief of tension resulting from the cutting. This behavior represents a sudden obsessional thought about relieving tension by cutting and then a compulsive action of the cutting itself. The cutter never understands (does not know) what it's all about. *No insight!* With insight, with discussing the meaning of it all and then with the struggle to overcome the acting-out based upon such insight, shortcuts of the psyche (cutting representing some fulfilled wish albeit in perverse form) can be replaced with more mature behavior.

Thus, it could be said that the psyche has its own unidimensional personality which is always to try to reduce immediate and ongoing tensions of the personality—without regard to whether such a command of the psyche is actually good for the person or not. The psyche responds to a unidimensional proposition, and that is that to reduce immediate tension within the personality is to support the ego and thereby the person's sense of security and pleasure. The psyche (taking its orders from the pleasure principle) wants the wish (the pleasure principle's chief representative) to be gratified. With respect to the ego, a consistent wish concerns the aim of feeling comfortable—without tension.

Tension and the Nature of Anxiety

When referring to tension within personality functioning, we are essentially considering the nature of anxiety since anxiety is implicated in almost all of personality dynamics. Even though *tension* and anxiety are used interchangeably in everyday language, nevertheless as used clinically, tension usually refers to conflict in the sense that a feeling of opposing forces is straining or "stretching" the person (as in decision-making with respect to two differing values to follow). *Anxiety,* on the other hand is rather preferred as a clinical term because it contains implicit reference to misgivings regarding acts or impending acts as well as specifically connecting to psychological phenomena and to psychiatric diagnosis. For example, anxiety rather than simple tension is more closely related to panic and the presence of such anxiety also can be a cue that it is a transformational signal from *below*, from anger that is repressed and unconscious. In this respect the anxiety is seen to radiate up— out of repressed anger.

Anxiety affects and even determines a host of emotional, behavioral, as well as physical disturbances, and can interfere in the free and smooth functioning of a person's inner resources. Further, the presence of anxiety also frequently signals deeper problems such as a variety of pathologies (disorders) that may be plaguing the person.

The term *anxiety* is derived from the Greek word *agon*. And out of agon is derived "anguish" and "agony." Anxiety is also related to the German word *angst,* meaning something akin to existential "fear" or "terror." As a template for understanding psychological disorders, the use of the term *anxiety* was also historically considered to reflect any condition considered to be neurotic; that is, if the person experienced anxiety within the context in which no psychosis existed (no craziness), then this experienced presence of anxiety was a defining measure of perhaps an existing neurosis. In order to be diagnosed with a neurosis it was assumed that the person affected would display or admit to experiencing undue anxiety.

In the formation of personality, the presence of distressing anxiety has immediate effects. For one, such anxiety will affect a person's attention span, memory, and ability to tolerate frustration. In such cases, the person's capacity for patience becomes at least somewhat interfered with and, at most, downright impaired. Of course, the net effect of such impairment in the person's functioning is frequently seen in depressive and withdrawal reactions, school problems, job loss, loss of control over angry reactions, and difficulty in conducting relationships generally.

All the vicissitudes of anxiety will be crucial when considering acting-out behavior. Thus, deleterious effects of anxiety include considerations of whether the anxiety is acted out (doing impulsive or delinquent things), or acted in as in somatizing the anxiety (developing physical expressions such as physical symptoms). In both cases this sort of anxiety is probably not consciously experienced by the person but is rather converted to action represented by externalizing the anxiety (acting-out) or by internalizing it (acting-in). In either case, the psychological choice to manage the anxiety this way, rather than creating a more curative process, will ultimately support pathology.

The acting-out or acting-in is essentially a flight into action with what can be considered a counterphobic approach to the challenge of existing anxiety. This means that the anxiety is so threatening to the person that some kind of reflexive "flight" behavior takes place which in this case refers to countering the possibility that a lifting of repression may be threatening to occur so that the content of unconscious material might then surface into consciousness. In the sense of a person's discomfort or *tension* regarding this sort of possibility (the possibility of unconscious material becoming conscious), acting-out then undermines any sense that such *tension* would turn into a bona fide *anxiety* state. The person avoids such an *anxiety* state by impulsively fleeing into the acting-out behavior in order not to feel the *anxiety*. When the acting-out is successful, then the *tension* about it all is erased. The "tension about it all" refers to a rather undefined feeling that something might happen but does not have to happen; that is, that surfacing the unconscious material can be prevented by the acting-out or acting-in.

In contrast, a smoother formation of the personality in the absence of anxiety would enable the person to think through whatever problem is causing the tension. And this is the nub of the problem: When the person is able to think about the problem (thereby tolerating the presumed tension about it) because of reasonably good ego-strength, then any acting-out, or acting-in becomes far less possible, and so in the person's personality the various components of the personality can then form more normally. In such a case, the tension would not in all likelihood develop into bona fide anxiety that necessitates, for certain individuals, acting-out behavior.

Unfortunately, acting-out or acting-in does in fact have the effect, for all intents and purposes, of erasing anxiety. However, this is essentially fool's gold since the acting-out or acting-in behavior simply makes it more difficult for the personality to form more smoothly. Rather, such disordered behavior makes everything worse and creates in the psyche a need for the development of a symptom-process to accommodate the inability of the person to face whatever is the specific meaning of the anxiety.

With the person's reflexive response of suppressing or repressing the anxiety and thereby acting it out, the anxiety itself will not be experienced. As such, rather than a neurosis developing in which the experience of anxiety can lend itself to an analysis and perhaps a working-through toward smoother functioning, the person develops what is known as *character problems* (patterns of behavior minus anxiety), and at times also develops symptoms—all occurring so as not to experience anxiety.

Personality of the Psyche

Even though in reality the end result of the symptom of acting-out could, of course, create great problems for the individual acting-out, nevertheless, the experience of the acting-out behavior itself—during the act—is a courting of pleasure, and a utilitarian psychological attempt to avoid tension through the psyche's engineering of "a psychological trick" (the acting-out itself) that then recedes or lessens the person's apprehension or tension. Therefore, it can be said that the psyche is a psychologically based evolutionary construction engineered to service the pleasure principle but not necessarily containing the checks and balances of ethical and moral benchmarks. This phenomenon of the psyche is so arranged because the psyche only understands it is to protect the subject's ego even though at times such strategy may actually not be in the person's best realistic interest.

This is also the case in the psyche's use of defense mechanisms of the personality. These defense mechanisms, such as rationalization (giving oneself reasons/ excuses for motivation and behavior), projection (blaming on others what one doesn't want to see in oneself), and displacement (using surrogates in the repositioning of one's feelings onto these surrogates), are designed to manage emotions in the attempt to control tension and to short circuit the possibly growing formation of anxiety.

This idea of control over tension (and potential anxiety) brings us to the point where we need to examine the vital importance of this issue of control over tension (and potential anxiety) as a function of the psyche's work to calibrate the controls of the personality over impulses. This ratio of control versus impulse is crucial with respect to how such a ratio can affect personality organization.

The central issue in becoming a social being concerns how one is able to manage the yearning in the psyche to express impulses (on the spur of the moment) as one feels them (and as they want to be expressed), versus the extent to which individuals have internalized the ability to manage such impulses as well as managing the stress/tension that could be generated by keeping such impulses in check. The urge one has to express impulse in the face of the need to control it does indeed generate stress—and occasionally great stress. Therefore, within the personality management of impulse (vital to personality organization) occurs through the specific action of internalized controls.

It needs to be remembered that impulses and emotions "understand" only their own internal command. They are not subject to the social constraints of civilized living. For example, as mentioned earlier, fear only knows that it "wants" to flee, and anger only "knows" that it "wants" to attack. Therefore, the issue of controls as they develop and function becomes crucial to the understanding of personality formation.

In the following chapter, this issue of impulse and its relation within the personality to such internalized controls is examined.

CHAPTER FOUR

Impulse versus Control

W<small>E ARE CONCERNED</small> here with the idea that there is a crucial interplay between impulses in the personality that continuously strive for expression, compared to the resources available concerning the ability to use controls and regulation to manage such impulses. We need to remember that such impulses are akin to instincts and emotions, and are energized products of the psyche that contain arousal inclinations. These are the impulses of aggression, hostility (underpinned by anger), and sexuality. They are also accompanied by inclinations of impatience, impetuousness, urgent gratification needs, and general needs for release of tension.

When impulses are intense and begin to accumulate they then point the person in the direction of behavioral action-orientation (impulsive doing), which in turn vastly raises the probability that acting-out can occur. In addition, when impulse dominates, then it is a foregone conclusion that judgmental lapses and poor frustration tolerance will be characteristic of the person's motivation, decision-making, and behavior.

However detrimental to the person the acting-out impulse may be, nevertheless, such acting-out of behavior will reduce the person's anxiety (which is the aim of the psyche's engineering strategy in the first place). The problem is that even though a person can reduce overall tension through acting-out, it is just about always the case that the acting-out is a disordered product of the personality (often distinctly pathological), reflecting a disorder of the personality. This implies that although a reduction of general tension as well as an erasure of specific anxiety feels better, nevertheless, to sustain tension or anxiety is frequently necessary for problems to be faced and worked out.

Thus, in the formation of anyone's personality, the issue of which dominates, impulse or control, becomes central to the particular diagnostic style of the personality—as for example, whether the person will turn out to have a measure of an emotion-controlled style of personality or some measure of an emotion-*dyscontrolled* style, and whether the person can hold impulse in and utilize this holding for productive purposes.

It is true, that individuals who are relatively adaptable (and normally so), have a comfortable fluctuation in the interplay between impulse and control. It is important to have this variation or fluctuation because the impulse will always strive for expression while the person's controls are designed to manage and even oppose such expression. This kind of struggle between impulse and control yields the nature of the person's level and kind of general tension as well as the level and kind of specific anxiety.

The idea of normal functioning between impulse and control is for the person to develop an equilibrium (asymmetrical though it may be: more control, less impulse), despite occasional shifts where according to changing external situations, impulse sometimes dominates, or instead, controls dominate. In uncontrollable shifts, impulse will almost always dominate and acting-out probability will increase as positive functioning decreases.

The Impulses

It needs to be remembered that impulses have an urgent nature and therefore, when such impulses are acted upon (usually also urgently) it is likely that one's perception, thinking, and judgment will be negatively affected. Thus, the intrusion of impulse can affect the person's intellectual or cognitive operations to the point wherein such disturbance becomes knitted into the personality as proclivities and habits and then contribute to a dyscontrolled personality style. Of course, when controls dominate impulse then the person develops habits that become knitted into the personality accordingly, and contribute to a more controlled style of personality.

THE ANGER IMPULSE

Impulses of aggression, hostility, impatience, impetuousness, and the need to release impulse because of immediate needs for gratification are usually subsumed under the heading of anger impulses. And these also include fantasy rumination; that is, a continuing replaying of angry feelings in fantasy and their associated potential feelings and behaviors such as revenge, jealousy, hatred, competitive striving, domination, sarcasm, quarrelsomeness, and, even in compensatory behavior, in compulsively excessive achievement pursuits. The nature and level of a person's anxiety also can be viewed as a result of how the anger impulse is expressed: as a feeling, as a fantasy, or as in acting-out.

As such, and with respect to the formation of one's personality, it becomes important to know whether the anger is translated into fantasy and feelings of hostility (which will contain mental images), or instead, whether such anger is transformed into direct aggressive behavior and acting-out.

THE SEXUAL IMPULSE

The sexual impulse is a libidinous one that is also striving for gratification. It contains pleasure fantasies, power themes, as well as literal sexual fantasies. Such fantasies and power themes are designed in the person's psyche to mediate or manage anxiety regarding direct sexuality. The acting-out of sexual impulses includes excessive or compulsive masturbation, perversions, and promiscuity. Such acting-out of sexual impulses can also negatively affect judgment, planning ability, concentration, and memory. In a general sense, the inability or incapacity to manage sexual impulses in a reasonable or normal way also can dramatically interfere with one's ability to be introspective and to think through important issues of life.

The Controls

There is a maturity index that can be fashioned, which implies how the balance between impulse and control can be assessed. For example, it is clear that an impulse-dominated personality is, to whatever extent, immature, whereas a control-dominated personality is probably one that is better off. However, if the control-dominated personality is severely controlling, then that too can be considered immature. Therefore, a decent balance is needed to ensure that the personality will be one that can withstand pressures, that can delay gratifications instead of yielding to impulsive moments, and that in total, the ratio of impulse to control can be a viable and balanced one in order for the personality to be resilient and able to withstand the daily pressures of life.

Such a ratio between *impulse* and *control* will naturally mean that controls need to be better positioned and stronger in the personality than are impulses, and in addition, there needs to be a variety of controls so that the management of impulse can be gained from several points of advantage.

In the following, this array of controls derived from various facets of the personality will be defined.

Cognitive Controls: Cognitive controls (facets of thinking and intellectual elements) include the ability to concentrate and to be consistent in one's strivings, and in one's pursuit of goals. In this sense the person's aim to achieve is in line with the person's ability to implement activities that are aimed toward those goals. Cognitive controls are usually considered in terms of specific intellectual functions and capacities such as decent language development and a good ability to make distinctions—to discriminate what is considered poor judgment from good judgment.

Ego Controls: Mostly, the controls calibrated by the ego keep the person's equilibrium steady (control over impulse) and enable the person to continue to implement activity toward goals in a rather straightforward manner, and in the absence of any significant detours toward such goals. This also means that the ego function of control permits the person to experience frustration but in the face of it, to be able to tolerate such frustration and then correspondingly to delay necessary gratification for whatever period of time necessary.

Defense Mechanisms as Controls: Defense mechanisms are specifically designed in the psyche to manage, regulate, and control specific transitory (or quickly passing) emotions, including anxiety; and this function of the defense mechanism enables the person to deal with the emotion in a way that keeps it in reasonable expressive form rather than permitting the emotion to go haywire.

Character or Personality Traits as Controls: These are enduring patterns of control in the form of patterns of behavior, and they may be separated into configurations of active traits and passive traits. In compulsive-personality styles, active traits are seen whereas in passive styles, retreating traits are seen. Both types are designed to control anxiety. Successful control consists of patterns that bind the anxiety rather than allowing it to float freely. These patterns contain the following cluster of traits, some of which are relegated to the domain of controls whereas others are relegated to the domain of impulse. In each case, the design is for anxiety to be controlled:
   Traits that convert impulse into work – These are so-called sublimating traits of conscientiousness, responsibility, and industriousness.

Impulse traits – Including aggression and need for immediate gratification.

Pleasure-dominated traits – Including hedonism (pleasure seeking), magical thinking, sociability, and optimism.

Anger-dominated traits – Including aggressive and passive behavior, hostility, oppositionalism, defiance, stubbornness, quarrelsomeness, sullenness, and belligerence.

Fear-dominated traits – Including phobic reactions, caution, shame, timidity, self-consciousness, pessimism, and obedience.

Dependency-dominated traits – Including deference, dependency, and need for affection.

Fantasy as Controls: Mediates between feelings and behavior and involves thinking instead of behaving. Control occurs through grandiose feelings generated by fantasy. Success in such fantasy neutralizes anxiety.

Fear as Control: Includes appearance of phobia to control panic.

As can be seen, the source of controls for any person is derived from a number of places and, within the personality, far outstrip the biologically given numbers of impulses. Yet, the striving of the impulse for expression is so much a part of our genetic and biological make-up that it takes all of these sources of controls to establish the possibility of a greater balance between impulse and control as well as a more mature control of such impulses.

Therefore, in the process of the formation of one's personality, it can be seen that how controls manage impulses and anxiety, and how within the personality acting-out is moderated, will help determine whether any given person is more or less likely to develop either a personality style that is more emotion-controlled, or more emotion-dyscontrolled. Of course, the emotion-controlled types will have a ratio in favor of control over impulse, whereas the emotion-dyscontrolled types will display a ratio in favor of impulse over control.

In the following section, the issue of taming the impulses is understood as a particularly significant factor in the organization of personality. In effect, a decent ratio of controls over impulses affords the ongoing development of personality a tremendous assist. This is known as *assessing one's maturation level* to see whether as the formation of personality unfolds the various facets of holding it together—of keeping the developing personality together—is developing normally. More or less, this measure of whether such development is indeed forming normally is called *a maturation index.*

Maturation: An Index of Impulse versus Control

An abundance of impulses in the personality usually creates a reasonably valid sense that the developing personality of any individual is retaining strong immaturities rather than relinquishing these feelings and behaviors for more-mature development. In contrast, if the level of maturation increases in the sense of normal expectations, then the balance between impulse and control will calibrate in the favor of controls.

In addition, the opposite is also true insofar as when there is an overabundance of controls that more or less completely squash impulse, then this too reflects the development of, and greater stasis of, more immaturity—the effect of which is to keep healthy development in a less-than-normal cadence of development.

Immature: Impulse Dominated

Impulse elements of the personality cause the individual to be somewhat scattered, disorganized, and to have strong proclivities for action. In addition, such characteristics are highly correlated to less-than-a-good ability for tolerating frustration and therefore are also accompanied by stronger-than-usual needs for motoric expression (for moving around and not being so able to be still and calm as would be desired in age-appropriate ways).

With respect to the very important consideration of the ability one has to delay immediate needs for gratification, the immature and impulse-dominated individual will display a variety of evidence to suggest an inadequate ability for delaying gratifications for the purpose of supporting more longer-range goals that even in an objective sense would be in that person's better interest. Instead, satisfying desires and needs without delay become a typical expression of such an impulse-dominated person, of course testifying to a developmental index greater in immaturity values.

With respect to the highly important feature of one's personality, enabling a person to accomplish goals concerns the person's ability not to rely solely on magical wishing, thinking, and fantasy regarding such goals, but rather to be able to implement with effort and longer-range doing-activity—whatever is required over time actually to accomplish these goals. Of course with individuals who are characterized as immature and impulse-dominated, magical wishing becomes a typical way of managing anxiety, and the anticipation of work-effort as well as the ability to confront tensions and still manage to stave off frustrations in order to gradually accomplish these goals becomes an underdeveloped possibility. Scattered trial-and-error attempts are also typical of this sort of immature and impulse-dominated individual, and such scattered probes almost always cancel out what would be more-mature attempts at work-effort, which are usually accomplished through learning and via persistent effort.

The personal sense of power, therefore, that a mature individual would achieve through effort and persistence is nullified in the immature-impulsive personality, and in the place of such more-mature qualities one finds a plethora of magical thinking, wishing, as well as a high level of squandering time.

Immature: Control Dominated

When the person is almost entirely focused on over-control, then the immaturity that results is also a signal that the developing personality is being interfered with by needs that are pressing the individual to clamp down on what is perceived to be an unnecessary volume of underlying impulse—impulse that is perceived to be ultimately dangerous.

This sort of excessive control within the developing personality necessarily creates a need for the person to become more behaviorally inhibited. Inertia and passivity can be a result of such inhibition. Feelings of caution and apprehension also lobby the person to sustain all attempts at control. Such a person's expressive-behavior repertoire will be correspondingly affected negatively so that spontaneity and general adventurousness will be significantly diminished. In addition, usually compulsive and obsessive features as well as a rigid profile and restriction of social ease will also prevail when elements of controls are over-represented in the person's personality organization.

This sort of person does not have the capacity to channel impulses into behavior in a way that leads to gratification of goals. Rather, this kind of rigid and constricted control-aggregate is targeted solely to reduce any sense of danger associated with the possibility of the appearance and effect of impulse. Therefore, over-control actually represents an underdevelopment of more-mature constructive controls.

Mature Balance of Impulse and Controls

Clearly, the balance between impulse and controls needs to be such that it can be maximally adaptive. Such a balance would signal that the individual can in fact utilize inner resources of perception, thinking, feeling, and behavior in an integrative effective and mature manner. With this mature and balanced index of impulse and controls, the further development of the personality in its stages of forming gives itself the best possible chance to satisfy each level and stage of development in a way that does not at all retard forward progress.

Such a balance reflects greater resilience and flexibility along with a probable decent measure of the organization of defenses in the personality. The development of the entire defense system of the personality is usually seen as the centerpiece in the capacity and functioning of the person's ego—meaning the person's ability to manage tensions, to work effectively, to test reality accurately, and to be able to integrate in a grand orchestration: the varied features of the entire personality.

In the following chapter, an analysis of the defense system and its correlates and functions is presented. As mentioned, these defenses are inextricably important in the development and functioning of the personality.

CHAPTER FIVE

Defense Mechanisms

I T IS PROBABLY a good bet to assume that defense mechanisms were developed in evolution to address emotions and, therefore, specific defense mechanisms can be related to specific emotions. Yet, because the system of how the defenses are organized is so adaptive, then no matter how each mechanism of defense exists to govern each specific primary emotion, such defenses are also available to amalgamate into clusters of signature categories that can address any number of personality styles.

Therefore, the defense system in the personality can add to the ratio of control over impulse in two distinct ways. First, there are the individual as well as the cluster defenses that manage individual emotions; and second, there are the defenses involved in the development of character and personality traits and not solely relegated to manage specific emotion.

Individual Defenses

Compartmentalization — This defense reduces anxiety by keeping aspects of personality apart so that contradictions do not register. Dissociative Identity Disorder is targeted by this defense mechanism as is the histrionic personality style.

Denial — This defense wards off the possibility of perceiving anything negative about another person. It aids in the person's effort to receive only positive information. Denial is also frequently seen abetting the histrionic personality style.

Displacement — This is the mechanism chiefly utilized in the service of attenuating the emotion of anger. The person will direct blame, anger, and aggression to less-threatening substitute figures so that these emotions are not focused on the more threatening target that for any number of possible reasons is too threatening to confront.

Intellectualization — Emotion is avoided by means of a focus on intellectual concerns, and/or through the use of reason and problem solving. This defense is usually associated with obsessional or compulsive personality styles, and may also be part of a defense cluster including the defenses of isolation, rationalization, sublimation, and undoing. This defense cluster operates to manage the emotion of expectation or anticipation by controlling the environment and thereby minimizing any elements of surprise that could generate undue anxiety.

Isolation — Here ideas are kept separate from feelings and this defense is frequently seen in obsessive and compulsive personality styles.

Projection — Faults, feelings, and impulses that cannot be faced or tolerated in oneself are attributed to others. It is a defense chiefly observed in paranoid states but is ubiquitous throughout the personality constellations.

Rationalization — With rationalization as a defense, the person is able to engage in a justification process in which unacceptable motivations or behaviors are made acceptable and even tolerable through explanations that have the appearance of logic. This defense is observed often in individuals who can be characterized as obsessive and/or compulsive in their styles of relating.

Reaction-formation—The emotion of pleasure or attraction that may be intolerable is transformed into its opposite, which can then be accepted. Thus, in reaction-formation, emotion is turned into its opposite only if the original emotion contains a component of pleasure, which is considered threatening. This defense is especially targeted to manage the experience of sexuality, which is perceived as dangerous or in some other way as incorrect or as in a situation that should be prohibited. In such instances (in the appearance of reaction-formation) to address whatever is the interpersonal situation, the attraction (pleasure or sexuality) would be transformed into its opposite feeling—that of disgust or revulsion or agitation, or dissatisfaction. Along with the defense mechanisms of compensation and sublimation, this cluster of defenses is frequently utilized by a person who begins to experience manic episodes—largely as a defense against depression. It is the compensatory defense that defends against depressive urges, while the sublimation defense transforms the manic energy into work energy (explaining why the manic person can be involved in many projects), and finally, the reaction-formation enables the person to calibrate his or her pleasure response better so that such a response can be gratified as well through work and not through prohibitory sexual attractions that may threaten to become realized in sexual activity.

Regression — The use of this mechanism implies an immature level of functioning. In antisocial, psychopathic, or any other numbers of impulse disorders, the regression defense is chiefly responsible for the maintenance of *motoric behavior* (the person's need not to be still). If not for this defense in their experience, such a person would feel rendered without a sense of movement; rather, in the absence of regression, such a person would possibly feel a sense of emotional paralysis, immobility, and inhibition. This person's behavior (the behavior of the psychopath, for example), depending as it does on the regression defense, reflects success in the person's need to move around and create endless stimulation. It is akin to the child's need for the same kind of behavior, and the similarity to the child's need for stimulation and movement therefore accounts for the observation of immaturity in the characteristic personality style of such a person.

Repression — This is the common underlying element in all defense mechanisms since it involves the expelling and withholding of intolerable ideas and feelings from consciousness. Repression is particularly utilized to manage conscious-threatening feelings of fear and even terror. Yet, its less-visible and perhaps more-profound function is to erase from consciousness angry feelings toward some person who is responsible for thwarting one's wishes. The more pervasive this mechanism is in the personality, the greater the likelihood of passive, schizoid, or histrionic features in the personality style.

Sublimation — This defense mechanism is utilized by the psyche to moderate impulses involving aggressive and sexual urges by channeling such impulses into productive and goal-oriented activity. Such goal-oriented activity is considered to be socially valuable. The successful utilization of sublimation is a mature indication in the personality since it implies that the person will be able to tolerate frustration and delay gratification in the service of longer-term goals.

Undoing — This mechanism is designed to maintain the person's habitual state of being, and is typical of obsessional, paranoid, and compulsive states. Thus, new commitments that are made are always correspondingly "undone" or counterbalanced by their opposite. Examples are: the buyer's regret whereby a person needs to return anything purchased; hand-washing to erase the presence of undesirable urges; and, any kind of ritualistic behavior that occurs in response to feeling angry or rejecting toward another person.

In summary, these individual defense mechanisms of compartmentalization, compensation, denial, displacement, intellectualization, isolation, projection, rationalization, reaction-formation, regression, repression, sublimation, and undoing, are presumably each designed to address individual emotions and styles of relating, all of which in turn serve the purpose of managing the person's tension level and general anxiety. Essentially then, these defense mechanisms are emotion-coping devices and also serve the purpose of aiding in the control of impulses.

Another cluster of defenses serves a somewhat different purpose in the personality. These defenses become chiefly responsible in the formation of enduring personality-trait patterns and, consequently, such defenses are focused on the more stable and enduring aspects of the personality. They are presented in the following section.

Defenses Forming Character/Personality Trait-patterns

Identification — This mechanism, as it exists as an accompanying element in all the defenses contributing to the formation of enduring personality styles, is similar to how repression represents a common thread in supporting the psychological aims in the operation of all the individual defense mechanisms. Therefore, identification appears as this common component in all of the defenses that form personality trait-patterns, or what is clinically called the formation of *character patterns*. Through identification, the person will try to imitate the behavior as well as the attitudes of another idealized person (usually a parent), in order to establish a self-same identity that then mirrors the identity of the other idealized person. This enables one to self-regulate emotion and anxiety rather than depend on external constraints. This kind of mirroring occurs usually by example and not by instruction. In addition, such identification cannot be prevented. It occurs naturally and is implicit in the adage: "The apple doesn't fall far from the tree."

Internalization — The use of this mechanism is built on the foundation of the identification mechanism and adds the imprinting of values to the identification process. These values are then adopted with respect to standards of behavior along with the accrual of attributes of the mentoring figure. Regardless of one's intentions, one comes to feel controlled by the values of the mentor even though one's intellect and reasoning may "see it differently" or even see negative implications or conclusions to the presence of the mentor's values. Therefore even as an adult, when the inappropriate internalized standards from childhood are questioned, nevertheless, the emotional attachment to such values will still have a strong, although perhaps not permanent influence in the ongoing accumulation of trait-pattern development.

Projective Identification — With this defense, the person can attribute to others complex (negative) parts of the self that are repudiated by this self-same person. However, even in the face of such repudiation, the person will identify with such parts. *If you spot it you got it* could be an aphorism of this concept of projective identification. You may criticize someone for what you consider to be nefarious behavior. But if it haunts you, if it continues to boil your blood, it is suspect that some variant of projective identification may be operating. Although you may repudiate such behavior, it is possible that you may still identify with it. In the formation of trait patterns, projective identification enables the person to ignore difficult characteristics that are being built into the personality.

Splitting — Splitting is accomplished with the aid of compartmentalizations: One person can be considered all good while another is considered all bad. Such compartmentalizations are assisted by the elements of denial and displacement. This is frequently seen in the borderline-personality style where both positive and negative attributes are given to another, while because of such splitting, such a person ignores the contradiction. Therefore, conceptions of good and bad can be reversed without any sense of conflict or tension. For the borderline-personality type, splitting tends to erase potential problems of ambiguity and conflict and this becomes "a borderline signature" in this person's trait-pattern development.

Symbolization — Internal ideas and fantasies can become disguised through specific external representations or symbols. In this way, in the formation of trait patterns, distress can be avoided since everything becomes disguised in the process of internalizing what is desired.

Turning against the Self — Hostility is made more tolerable by turning it against the self. The person utilizing such a defense can develop traits of blaming, denigrating, and attacking the self instead of directing such feelings to the originally intended target. This originally intended target is usually someone who is important, but hostility toward that person is therefore hidden by the turning of the hostility against the self. Such a defense is frequently seen in masochistic individuals, or in those who self-mutilate.

In summary, I have tried to display the organization of defense as it exists in personality styles and types insofar as such defenses play a role in managing individual emotions as well as ensuring the development of personality or character trait-patterns. The central defense of repression in the management of emotion was seen as analogous to the central defense of identification in the formation of these personality trait-patterns.

In terms of how a personality forms, therefore, it is essential to consider these core issues of the psyche that begin to shape the ultimate configuration of one's personality in terms of one's diagnosis, and personality type and style. These core issues consist of the mechanics of controls within the personality and how such controls manage the considerable urges of impulses, along with how mechanisms of defense operate both to manage and calibrate transitory emotion (emotions that quickly come and go), as well as anxiety, and at the same time utilize another type of defense to manage the development of enduring trait-patterns in the personality—those personality characteristics by which people identify us.

In the following chapters of part 2, each of these basic types is organized with respect to how emotion is managed. Is emotion managed through control of the emotion, through release of the emotion, through fortifying an emotion-attached need, or through fortifying an emotion-detached need?

Each of the basic types along with their behavioral styles will also be provided with actual clinical examples. Within these clinical illustrations we will also be able to see clusters of personality traits as they are correlated to emotion and impulse. In addition and importantly, these basic personality styles will be placed on a continuum so that we will be able to see such styles easily, more or less in their normal form, as well as seeing these exact styles in a form that might be considered distressed or even emotionally and mentally disturbed.

PART TWO

The Basic Personality Styles

Basic personality styles are designed to calibrate tension in distinctly defined ways. Four categories of such personality styles are considered whereby the management of tension is achieved by a corresponding management of emotion; typically by controlling emotion as in Emotion-controlled Styles, or typically by assuring that emotion is not controlled as in Emotion-dyscontrolled Styles, or by keeping emotion in compliance with the caregiver, as in Emotion-attached Styles, or by limiting emotion as in Emotion-detached Styles.

Category 1
Emotion-controlled Styles

Emotion-controlled Styles of the personality are designed to prevent the feeling of being overwhelmed by the unexpected. Such persons sense that emotions can create a feeling of disorganization in the personality, and then involuntarily these emotions can go out of control. Therefore the control of emotion is perceived as an opportunity to feel safe and secure.

Because of the need for such control, those personality types that fit this sort of configuration (or style) rely on defense mechanisms that utilize logic, rationalization, and any other such method of defense that tend to create insularity or protection in social or interpersonal situations. The insulation of the personality then aids in controlling emotion.

Control of emotion, control of emotion, control of emotion is the mantra for such emotion-controlled types of the:

1. Obsessive-compulsive Personality
2. Paranoid Personality
3. Schizoid Personality

CHAPTER SIX

The Obsessive-compulsive Style

T HE OBSESSIVE-COMPULSIVE STYLE is designed primarily to control tension and emotion. As such, this person uses all sorts of intellectual defense mechanisms in order to circumvent and especially prevent the unexpected. The defense mechanism of intellectualization (reasoning) is used to support every position and attitude. Other such defenses include rationalization (creating a good reason for any act) and sublimation (expending an excessive amount of energy on tasks, thus leaving less energy for the possibility of sharing in relationships). In this sense, the greatest pleasure is derived from work, and in the working on projects and tasks (including making lists of things to do), thereby subtracting energy for any subsequent possible pleasures from relationships.

Thus, the focus on work leaves little or much-less time for the pursuit of friendships. Such a person needs to arrange his or her environment so that everything can be controlled. In this sense, the person inordinately begins to value orderliness, focuses on detail, and demands perfectionism in self and in others. This perfectionistic orientation can be so insistent that in a counterintuitive way it can begin to interfere in the person's ability to complete tasks: this, in the face of a strong need for closure. That is, such a person craves the perfect completion of the task. In extreme cases and on the one hand, such a person's perfectionism may interfere with completion of tasks; and, on the other hand, and at the same time, this person's need for closure (to complete tasks) continues to be challenged to the paradoxical extent that, frequently, tasks remain incomplete. A result of such conflict can be seen in the example of such a person's attempt to study for an exam. The textbook will be neatly underlined in various colors of felt-tipped pens, but the content of the material will not be learned. It is "form" that begins its insidious triumph over "content" simply because it is the orderliness that controls anxiety as well as controlling the overall pressure of emotion, rather than, or in place of, the expenditure of energy in the learning of the material.

Correspondingly, this person's standards can be so high that an over-conscientiousness develops, which begins to amount to a sort of moralism. It is a moralistic stance that becomes mostly concerned with the right and wrong of things to the extent that the person becomes inflexible. Thus, it is the rules and regulations that begin to count instead of the interaction and relationship with others. In this sense also, such a person can become rigid and even quite stubborn—qualities that become undermining when expressed in a relationship so that warmth and spontaneity are usually compromised.

With this picture in mind, it is rather clear that such a person will demand adherence—finding it difficult to delegate authority to others unless those others comply exactly with this person's idea of what it is that needs to be done—and how it should be done. This kind of demand leaves little room for discussion or alternatives and essentially is a miserly approach to sharing. As a matter of fact, such a person usually becomes miserly and can hoard anything of value; for example, in money.

The obsessive quality of this emotion-controlled style is the tendency to thought-repetition as in continuing to think about the same thing. The compulsive quality is the ritualistic "doing" of whatever "drivenness" or impulse "to 'do'" resulted from the repetitive thought.

Such thinking, leading to "doing" becomes a clinical odd-ity when the thinking turns into repetitive obsessional thought, which then leads to an irresistible need to actually go ahead and do something that addresses and satisfies the thought (a compulsive act).

Case Examples

Case 1: An obsessive-compulsive personality – A Symptom Sketch
A physician who held an important hospital post began feeling hostility to his chief of service. This hostility gradually became a preoccupation, and its repetitive occurrence also gradually became quite obsessional. The obsessional thought was that this physician noticed he was having an urge to gaze upon corpses. At some point, his obsessional thought to gaze at the corpses became exceedingly urgent. Whenever such thoughts gripped him, and in order to avoid the obsession, this physician would try to think different thoughts but he was not successful in doing so.

Eventually, he was in such an obsessional grip of the thought to gaze at corpses that one day the impulse to do so broke through the wall of *thinking* and into the action of *doing*. He then took himself to the pathology department of the hospital and began his gazing at these corpses that were in various stages of dissection.

Through a series of psychotherapy sessions, the physician discovered that his thinking and his behavior (his obsessive-compulsive act) to want to gaze at the corpses, and then actually to do it, was his unconscious wish that each corpse would be his chief of service. Therefore, he kept on thinking (obsessing) and going to discover (compulsively "doing") so that symbolically his entire wish for his chief of service actually to be dead was, over and over again, being satisfied simply by his gazing at the corpses.

The analysis of this physician's entire relationship with his chief of service revealed the presence of a great deal of stored-up anger, much of it quite suppressed or even repressed. With the analysis having the ring of truth, the physician steeled himself to talk to this chief of service, and in short order they resolved the conflict.

As a result, the obsessional thinking about the chief and especially his acting-out of visits to the pathology department ceased entirely.

This of course only demonstrates the symptom of an obsession and a compulsion. In contrast, the following illustration offers a glimpse of the true makeup of an obsessive-compulsive personality.

Case 2: An Obsessive-compulsive Personality

The typical example offered of the obsessive-compulsive personality is of the person who continues to check the locks on the door before bedtime, and then even after getting into bed, begins to ruminate about whether in the checking of the lock to see if it was actually locked, perhaps in error, rather than finally attempting to lock the lock, it was really unlocked.... Then, of course, the obsession turns into a compulsive feeling of again needing go and check the lock. This repetitive checking of the lock will occur a number of times so that it even becomes ritualistic; that is, that before the person can feel comfortable, it becomes necessary to go through the gauntlet of doubt and then gradually to resolve such doubt through a lot of tedious "doing."

In terms of personality characteristics, or personality traits, such an individual is generally perfectionistic, seeks orderliness, is interested in following rules and regulations, and is over-conscientious, thereby needing to stick to high standards of activity in a rather rigid adherence to habit. Such a person is interested in controlling all impulse and emotions including those of anticipations. Concern with parsimony and all of its variations, as well as concern with self-doubt occupy much of such a person's time.

The More Normally Inclined Obsessive-compulsive Style

In the more severe emotion-controlled nature of the obsessive-compulsive, the need for closure (needing to finish something that is unfinished and that needs completion) becomes a compulsive imperative. This kind of craving for completion (closure) begins to prevail forcefully and triumph over any other consideration of the person's life. In addition, various tasks and demands revolve around the need for everything to be quite perfect.

In contrast, more normally inclined obsessive-compulsive types direct their critical and perfectionistic energies toward very good planning as well as strategic and tactical ways of apportioning work so that the obsessive fantasy life and the compulsive impulses accompanying such thinking does not overwhelm the personality. Rather, the very good planning and strategy used by such a person keeps such fantasies and impulses in a secondary position while realistic evaluations about one's life and the apportionment of time is therefore usually not compromised. In this sense, such an emotion-controlled type can be quite a good relationship partner even though the person's basic nature is to control emotion as a way of limiting anxiety. It is in this sense, that the pathology that can accompany the obsessive-compulsive style is relatively absent. Rather, characteristics of such a type can be used to be quite efficient and productive. It is the kind of person who, with proper concentration, can study and learn material efficiently rather than spending time valuing the neat underlining of everything while not learning anything. In such cases even though a concern with self-doubt does in fact exist, its voltage is less than in more severe cases, so that the self-doubt would probably not utilize an undue amount of psychic energy.

CHAPTER SEVEN

The Paranoid Style

THE PARANOID STYLE is one in which distrust of the world, and how this distrust is played out, is the way such a person manages to achieve control over emotion. This kind of a person is suspicious and highly critical toward anyone and anything (other than the self). Underneath it all, the person is kind of saying to the self:

What is wrong is always out there in the world,
but never here, in me.

This is essentially the universal paranoidal theme. In this respect, the paranoid person (non-psychotic type), blames everything on the outside in order never to see what is actually and unconsciously viewed as wrong with the inside—the self. Ironically, what is unconscious for such a person is the feeling that everything is wrong with the self. To not want to see this explains the paranoid's need to be critical toward everything but the self. Therefore, what the paranoid person is really unconsciously saying to the self is:

Everything is wrong with me, in here, rather than
everything being wrong out there in the world.

Thus, the paranoid person is highly critical toward everything and this criticism is always projected outward. In this way, a sharp distinction is made between self and others; that is to say, there is always something wrong with the other person, but as stated, never with the self. It is this distinction between self and others that enables such a person to be in complete control of emotion. This control is always in the service of never being able to see one's own feelings of inadequacy. The main objective in such a person's strategy is to keep all feeling of inferiority repressed and out of consciousness.

Such a person distrusts the loyalty of others and is thus consistently suspicious. Of course, because of such a colossally sensitive ego, this sort of person can be emotionally wounded quite easily. And then, because of such hypersensitivity to any even negatively implied comment related to the self, the paranoid person will harbor grudges for any perceived slight, and then harbor these grudges forever. In addition, the anxiety that will result from experiencing a negative comment about the self will also usually provoke a counterattack.

Needless to say, such a person finds it extremely difficult to make friends, and is quite cautious in any even potential friendship. Rather, the paranoid person will demonstrate traits such as stubbornness, jealousy, hostility, sarcasm, cynicism, argumentativeness, along with an absence of warmth and humor, and in addition, usually will show an obvious rigidity in the personality. The function of this rigidity serves primarily to prevent the person from being controlled by others.

In the quest not to be controlled by others, such a person will also always be in a blaming mood, and will be preoccupied with scanning and scrutinizing the environment in order to identify and verify negative impressions of the world. This attitude is referred to as *guarded* and reflects the paranoid person's store of hostility toward others, which is turned around so that it feels to this person as though such hostility is incoming—from the world. The entire projection dynamic of such a paranoid person was what created the adage of paranoid projection in the first place—"If you spot it, you got it." This means that because such a paranoid person is so acutely aware of what are considered the nefarious threats in the world, it then correspondingly means that such diabolical and odiously evil intentions are really housed within the personality of that same paranoid person.

In addition, this perceived threat from the world is, of course, an exaggerated sense of vulnerability about the self, which in turn is denied by the self. Rather than feel and therefore act vulnerable, such a person uses an offense as the best defense, and proceeds to continue to criticize, condemn, and blame.

The main defense used by such a person is what is known as *projection;* that is, to attribute to others what is true of you. In this case, what this means is that the paranoid person finds imperfections all over the place—in the world—in order, as stated, not to see such imperfections in the self. However, the basic truth is that, in a very deep way, such a person sees the self as profoundly imperfect, and therefore subject to maximum criticism. However, this sense of the imperfect self is entirely unconscious so that this kind of person can continue to criticize and therefore continue to feel gratified by success of the criticism toward others; that is, the satisfaction of the criticism is in its very expression. In this way, the inferior sense of self correspondingly continues to be concealed—especially from the self, while all the faults and imperfections are attributed to the outside—to the world.

This is a personality that, in the absence of consciously knowing it, nevertheless harbors in the unconscious mind a real justification for the self to be blamed for all sorts of inadequacies and inferiorities. It is this basic critical sense of the self that is at the core of the paranoid person's need to be sure to control all emotion except in the use of blame and criticism toward others. The implication is that if emotion triumphs over control, then one cannot be sure that what is in the unconscious will stay in the unconscious. Thus, without control over emotion the fear is that whatever is in the unconscious will almost certainly escape into consciousness, and that would be the worst possible scenario for such a person.

Case Examples

Case 1: A Paranoid Personality – A Symptom Sketch

A thirty-nine-year-old man was reasonably normal in most of his life except that he was frequently troubled by the thought that people might be looking at him and even following him with the intention of robbing him. This man was never married, was socially somewhat of a loner, and reported being lonely. It was evident that his social isolation was not something he craved. Rather, because of his somewhat difficult personality—he was frequently critical of those with whom he worked—apparently, people were not drawn to him.

The analysis of his fear of being followed and robbed revealed what is known as *an encapsulated paranoid* feature of his personality. This essentially means that altogether he was not psychotic or even significantly abnormal in his everyday life, but that whatever disturbance he did have, was housed in "a bubble" by his so-called fear of perhaps being followed and robbed.

In addition, the analysis revealed a most surprising although not unusual interpretation. Underneath it all, in his unconscious mind, his wish was actually the opposite of being followed and robbed; that is, he wanted to follow, and yes, wanted also (in a way), to rob others. And this so-called surprising interpretation was based on the obvious—he needed contact, and wanted something they had (regarding the issue of riches; that is to say, companionship riches). Basically, he needed companionship. So, it was this issue of the riches of companionship that related to what was missing in his life. Underneath it all, he didn't want to be alone and yet was never conscious of this need.

In this encapsulated-paranoid symptom, this man who underneath it all only wanted *not* to be alone, could not help doing things that accomplished just the opposite: exhibiting rejecting behavior toward others that ultimately and consistently assured his loneliness.

Case 2: A Paranoid Personality

In discussing the paranoid personality, we are not referring to paranoid schizophrenia in which such a person would be having either delusions of persecution ("people are poisoning me"), or delusions of grandeur ("I am God"), or both, and where, in addition, such a person also may even have hallucinations. In such cases of psychosis, the person's sense of reality is profoundly compromised so that what counts is what they believe, and not what is objectively happening around them.

In contrast, the paranoid personality considered here is someone who is critical, oppositional, envious, jealous, and suspicious. It is a person who listens more to internal needs and is only interested in personal comforts.

Such a person was a woman of seventy. She was someone who could not abide any sort of advice or suggestion that was different from what she thought was right. In other words, everything about what she thought, had, or did, was considered by her to be okay, and what other people thought really didn't matter to her. Her daughter would constantly tell this woman that her stockings were tattered or had runs, and that she had stains on her blouse, or that she was rude to someone. The daughter indicated that her mother would criticize everyone but never could accept suggestions about improving herself. This woman's answer would be that her blouse was clean, so that the stain that was showing was a permanent one and since the blouse was laundered then the stain didn't matter despite her daughter's comment about how a stained blouse is usually not socially acceptable. She would add that even though her nylons had a visible run in them, nevertheless they were functionally perfectly wearable.

In this case, the woman was entirely unable to accept a kind of comment that in any way pointed to an imperfection that she might be displaying. Yet, she was constantly focusing on what she considered to be everyone else's imperfections. In addition she was usually interested in information about other women she knew, and would feel annoyed and even jealous if she felt they had something that she considered to be valuable or of a nature that bestowed a certain prestige to the other person.

All in all, this woman was this way for most of her life. She was married for less than a year before the marriage was annulled. In that time, she became pregnant and her daughter reported that this woman was constantly competitive with the mothers of her daughter's friends, insisting always that these other mothers were lacking in intelligence or commonsense especially concerning the issue of raising children. Essentially, this person needed to be right all the time and could not tolerate feeling she was wrong about anything.

In this example of, more or less, a lifelong paranoid personality, the aim of the personality constellation was to keep all of her emotion contained and controlled, and to engage in all sorts of thinking and behavioral maneuvers that acted to see the entire world as deficient and therefore imperfect, whereas she herself remained pristine in every way—the stains on her blouse, notwithstanding.

The More Normally Inclined Paranoid Style

A receded paranoid style, or a person who is not pathologically paranoid but still in all reflects a paranoid caution, can be considered quite able to be a partner in an interpersonal relationship.

Despite such a person's need to control emotion as an adaptive way to live life, nevertheless this type does not need to operate with the serious cluster of paranoid characteristics such as persecution expectations or experience of world-salvation grandiosity, or of expressing an unrelenting criticality toward the world. In addition, such a person will not be particularly envious and similarly will not necessarily be reflexively jealous, or oppositional, or particularly suspicious.

In contrast, there can exist a so-called more normal paranoid inclination enabling such a person possibly to partake of and even enjoy companionship, as well as having the ability to make and sustain friendships. More than average caution, and a refined sense of distinctions, are readily made that permit this person to see the unpleasant conditions of the world, and these characteristics of a refined proclivity to make distinctions could definitely identify this paranoid inclination, but such a person would not be squandering significant time by constantly pointing fingers in order to feel gratified in the assessment that everything is wrong.

Thus, in this type of emotion-controlled type, essential and profound paranoid thinking is eschewed in favor of more normal functioning although a definite inclination toward caution as well as the impulse to assess everything retains its latent existence. The need to evaluate every little thing distinguishes this more-normally inclined person from the more-serious paranoid personality. In both cases, however, the caution about accepting anything "new" does in all likelihood exist. However, in the more normally inclined paranoid individual, resistance to "the new" is far less potent. It is actually a matter of degree.

CHAPTER EIGHT

The Schizoid Style

THE SCHIZOID PERSONALITY is defined as one in which an aloofness, remoteness, and withdrawal characterizes the overall demeanor of the person. It is this rather distant and unemotional attitude that enables the person to control emotion and tension. Emotion frequently emerges as somewhat cold, and flat (a monotone). This personality style however, is not of the schizophrenic type. In this Schizoid Style, the person is free of any hardcore diagnostic psychotic syndrome or psychotic pattern.

Such a person however, is usually without close relationships so that a noticeable social detachment corresponds to the person's emotional restriction. The result is a profile of a person who is quite self-contained, and who thus avoids close relationships. The usual qualities of warmth and reciprocity that make up the components of social bonding are absent here. Rather, this person usually chooses solitary activities, has few if any friends, and is typically without sexual contact.

The net effect of the detached, distant, and solitary social structure inherent in this schizoid style is that because such a person only develops limited numbers of relationships, at best, such a person may have three or four such attachments in a lifetime— one or two of which are parents. And if, perchance, another person pressures a friendship, the schizoid person will then experience greater tension and may very well seek to avoid the relationship or potential relationship entirely.

The fantasy life of such a person is heavily represented with hostile themes as well as with compensatory fantasies. What this means is that such a person will make up, in fantasy, what is lacking or missing in reality. For example, it is said that such a person can be rather immune to compliments and/or criticism. Yet, an analysis of such a person's fantasy life reveals an actual and strong sensitivity to criticism, insofar as in the fantasy life images of "getting even" is an excellent illustration of such concern about, and sensitivity to, criticism. In addition, because of the amount of time spent in fantasy, it becomes obvious that a person who exhibits this sort of schizoid style, gains a great deal of personal gratification from such an active life of fantasy—especially in the sense of such fantasies containing the theme of anger around which is constructed the story context of the fantasy. As a matter of fact, with respect to gaining gratification this sort of person derives the greatest amount of personal gratification from such fantasies characterized by compensatory themes as well as by themes of revenge.

This person's defensive structure consists mostly of intellectualized defenses such as rationalization and compartmentalization. Compartmentalization means that the person sections off parts of his life so that there are rather thick barriers between life's different arenas. This sort of compartmentalized defense permits emotion to be controlled insofar as the particular defensive structure limits the kind of events that could surprise the person; that is to say, that in this person's attempt to control emotion, the element of feeling surprised by events or by the unexpected, needs, if possible, to be kept to a minimum.

Furthermore, because this person attempts to control the environment by being remote and aloof, then fantasy can take over. In such a circumstance, in which fantasy becomes dominant, from time to time such a person may lose the gift of good judgment.

This less-than-adequate judgment results from the inordinate time spent in withdrawal and fantasy—thinking and imagining. Yet, for the most part, a person who is characterized by the Schizoid Personality Style is usually logical as well as analytical.

In addition, the chief mechanism of defense utilized by such a person is called *isolation of affect*. Isolation of affect simply means that the person is able to parse any emotion—to isolate it—so that the emotion does not have the typical effect that an emotion usually has. That is to say, the emotion when isolated like that cannot make the person feel whatever it is that such a particular emotion generally gets a person to feel. To support this isolation of affect, such a person also utilizes the defensive mechanism of "suppression of affect." This means that in the use of suppression of affect, the isolation of emotion is better guaranteed because in such suppression a good deal of emotional intensity is subtracted (diluted) from conscious experience.

Case Examples

Case 1: A Schizoid Personality – A Symptom Sketch
A chemical engineer had an intact marriage for fifteen years. He had two daughters, was almost entirely functional in life (had a good job, was a reasonably good husband and was a concerned father). Nevertheless, he was noticeably remote with others and therefore socially detached from them.

This sort of emotional restriction and social remoteness corresponded to his need to control emotion because he felt that spontaneous social engagement (out-and-out fun) increased the possibility that he could say or do things that would seem to others to be immature or out of place. In this sense, this man was never sure about how he would be seen with respect to what he said or did. Over many years, his solution was to develop ways of avoiding social contact outside of his family. To his so-called friends he definitely seemed like an emotionally unavailable person even though he was able to develop his career (hold down a job and have a family). He was able to be married because a childhood classmate of his pursued him. To him, she didn't seem overly strange and he apparently was able to create a life with her. Therefore, he would need to be considered as an encapsulated schizoid personality so that he could live reasonably normally but in a bubble only with his family.

Case 2: A Schizoid Personality

A forty-five-year-old male postal employee was recommended for psychotherapy treatment by his supervisor because of a case of social under-responsiveness. This was a man who, with respect to his duties, was perfectly able to function on the job, but was not at all able to have easy and typical social interaction with his fellow employees. Yet, he was apparently responsible and conscientious.

Accordingly, he obeyed rules and regulations and was obedient and compliant to authority. He was also obviously quite intelligent. His way of gaining social gratification was in his activities with his family, his aged parents. In addition, he was quite an active reader of stories in books and magazines, and also had an active fantasy life in which he played the hero as well as the avenger. His favorite role was as avenger. The fact that in his fantasy life he was preoccupied with those people who did him wrong, meant that he needed to avenge the wrongs and this pointed to a degree of hostility that was being kept suppressed and controlled by the psychological organization of the his schizoid personality.

This man's social distancing behavior was his overall and general way to control and contain his emotional life and, more specifically, it was his way to contain his anxiety. His absence of warmth toward others, especially in his work environment did not at all mean that he was a malicious person. It just meant that he was an insulated and self-sufficient person whose isolation of emotion kept him feeling stable and safe.

The More Normally Inclined Schizoid Style

Rather than the pathology of the true schizoid type that includes a cluster of traits largely represented by social detachment (and more specifically including a self-containment along with the avoidance of close relationships), this syndrome will also be characterized by the person's total gratification through fantasy, usually composed of hostile themes. In addition, such a person resists surprises (because taken by surprise indicates absence of control), and shows considerable isolation of emotion. Another glaring and defining condition of such a type is an overly sensitive reaction to criticism.

In contrast, this schizoid inclination can also be seen in a person whose emotion-controlled style is only expressed minimally, and such a person can actually achieve important vocational and professional positions. In such cases, although these social contacts may be minimal (even superficial), nevertheless they do operate to provide all sorts of interactions, and such social contacts carry the assumption that this moderated schizoid person will indeed interact socially. Because of this interactional element in such a person's life, the preference to be entirely aloof and remote does not reach threshold so that withdrawal is less, and the person's emotional tone not as flat as might be expected in a classic schizoid condition.

In addition, because of such increased social interaction, such a person's fantasy life is far less infused with hostile themes. Therefore, whereby the more serious condition of the schizoid type cannot really be companionable in any conventionally easy manner, this more normal type with schizoid inclinations indeed can be more companionable even though that to nurture close relationships might still be difficult. In addition, such a person is not so concerned about resisting surprises simply because, in this benign schizoid state, extreme vigilance is absent, and this absence of extreme vigilance is correlated to the difference between a severely schizoid individual versus one that is less severe. In the less-severe type, an acting-out probability of hostility is just about nonexistent. In the more severe type, tense situations in which there is a demand to socialize or to answer to critical authority can significantly increase the probability of hostile acting-out: of aggression.

•   •   •

Category 2
Emotion-dyscontrolled Style

Emotion-dyscontrolled Styles are those in which the person is chiefly concerned with making sure that emotion does not get controlled. In this way, such individuals are usually involved in activities that tend to invite and instigate continuously stimulating events in the environment in order for emotion to be able to be released and not controlled. With events and activities swirling around them, such persons actually feel safe and secure because in the moments of activity, emotion tends to remain free from control.

No control over emotion, no control over emotion, no control over emotion, could be considered the mantra for such emotion-dyscontrolled styles of the:

1. Histrionic (Hysterical) Personality
2. Narcissistic Personality
3. Psychopathic (Antisocial) Personality

CHAPTER NINE

The Histrionic Style
(Hysterical)

THIS KIND OF person exhibits an excessive emotionality. Such excessive emotionality is frequently expressed in terms of exaggerated and dramatic displays of behavior. For example, such a person will recount a story or life event with great flourish and color. Yet, the emotionality is frequently shallow (only serving momentary needs), and in addition is usually highly changeable. An example of this shifting or changing of emotion can be seen when the person can become happy and then in a split second, also feel petulant if something desired is denied. In addition, such individuals will exaggerate what they describe as their intimate friendships and so-called closeness with others. This kind of exaggerated claim of social bonding is considered by even the most tolerant listener to reflect an immaturity.

As with all types of the Emotion-dyscontrolled Styles, hysterical or histrionic individuals actually need to be excitable and so they are usually involved in creating endless externally stimulating situations. This means that they provoke, invoke, evoke, and invite all sorts of activity, situations, conditions, and circumstances for the sake of creating excitement and stirring-up everything around them. All of this kind of activity permits the person to be over-active, emotional, and most of all, it rules out the possibility of being alone and solitary.

Aloneness and remoteness are conditions that the histrionic person will do anything to avoid. That is to say, with such alone-ness the inner life of the person begins to feel somewhat threat-ened. Since such individuals always will find it difficult to delay gratification, then the pressure to create stimulating conditions also serves the purpose of gratifying needs most immediately, and thereby the boredom-demon is avoided and the person feels free of threat.

In addition, people who react with this emotionally charged histrionic personality style are also found to be dependent on oth-ers who they hope (and even expect) will do the hard work. That is, they are extremely wishful, and therefore want others to solve problems and otherwise to join in the magical wish for satisfactory solutions to problems. For example, if the person wishes to lose weight, a distinct inability to do so becomes evident and there-fore such a person also becomes essentially unable to undertake or implement any sort of diet and/or exercise regimen. Instead, this person would want someone else to implement the diet and exercise regimen and actually (again, wishfully) lose the weight for them. Thus, the histrionic person is also one who has strong wishes, and puts great stock in thinking that such wishes need to be realized—it is hoped in a magical way. Such wishing also expresses obvious passivity.

This wishful orientation reveals the strongest general charac-teristic of the fantasy life of such individuals. This very strong general characteristic of the fantasy life contains a profoundly intense wish-system that harbors the need for solutions to occur, of course, magically. This means that in addition to the passivity, such a person is actually extremely dependent, seems helpless, and in addition, in order to sustain such a magical wish for successful solutions, the defense of denial is brought to bear on whatever the situation might be. In the use of this defense of denial, such a person screens in only what might gratify the wish, and screens out whatever might seem to be disappointing regarding the wish. In this sense of relying on one's wishes instead of assessing the reality of things, such a person's judgment frequently turns out to be less than adequate. Because of such shaky judgment, or judgment lapses, frequent difficulties arise for this person—typically in the form of a series of decisions that basically are undermining rather than helpful.

Such undermining acts (due to questionable judgment) invite many failure experiences so that this person will need constant reassurance, and as a result will surely overvalue praise. This kind of reassurance to such a person elevates the ego and serves a compensatory function (builds the person up), and thereby circumvents or prevents any depression from gaining traction. With depression avoided, such a person can then devote more time to gratifying fantasies. Sometimes, in the face of needs that are not automatically met, such individuals complain of physical weakness, and as a result will even crave or require bed rest. It is an old-time neurasthenia characterized by feelings of fatigue and lethargy.

The time spent in fantasy in this histrionic type is more specifically occupied mostly with romantic fantasies. These romantic fantasies are also frequently tinged with sexually explicit scenarios. Correspondingly in real life, such individuals are also sexually seductive, involved in physical displays for attention, and are usually exclusively attention-seeking. Such individuals are also usually coy, and typically behave in an extremely entitled manner. A flamboyant physical appearance is also characteristic.

The cardinal feature of such a histrionic personality style is the tendency toward high suggestibility. This high index of suggestibility makes such a person much more susceptible to being hypnotized (due to the uncritical stance and the high potential level of suggestibility). This is in contrast to the emotion-controlled style of the obsessive, or paranoid, or schizoid, who would be difficult to hypnotize because of a highly critical, controlled stance and the absence of a pointedly susceptible level of suggestibility.

With respect to this histrionic person's overall or general approach to the world therefore, it is an impressionistic style designed to release emotion rather than one that focuses on detail by implementing control over emotion. Thus, how this person feels emotionally (Emotion-dyscontrolled Style) is most important and is given value when emotion is released; whereas in contrast or in comparison, hard reality (as in the appropriate control over emotion) is relegated to secondary status only because such cold, hard reality may not correspond to what such a person wishes, wants, needs, or feels.

Case Examples

Case 1. The Histrionic (Hysterical) Case – A Symptom Sketch
A sixty-year-old married woman was constantly seeking romantic moments with men. In her experience of it all, a romantic moment was defined as any interaction with a man that could be considered a response to her flirtatiousness, or her perception of a man's flirtatiousness to her, or some actual verbal sexually suggestive interfacing, or generally anything that could be defined as personal interest that gets conveyed one person to the other.

This woman needed to engineer this sort of encounter at any and all given opportunities and when the circumstance didn't lend itself to such a possibility, she would feel either bored or irritable and then she would create some sort of difficulty with her husband. This kind of friction with her husband seemed to satisfy her need to blame him for what she felt was the absence of interest in life resulting from the corresponding absence of circumstance in which she could express her attractiveness to men and then expect that they, in turn, would respond to her the same way.

This particular symptom of hers was the outstanding element of her hysterical personality that needed constant stimulation from the outside world which, in this case called for a dramatic exhibitionistic display of flirtatious searches. It was such searches and perhaps their ostensible successful achievement that seemed to offer this woman a sense of security. Perhaps even more important was that this sense of security acted as reassurance that she was still attractive, but more specifically, it was essential evidence for her that she was an acceptable person to the world.

To her, evidence of acceptability in the world means the ability to have her emotional life on the ready at all times so that she could feel the necessary dyscontrol of emotion as an ingredient in her quest for romantic conquest and in her desire to feel well.

Case 2: The Histrionic (Hysterical) Personality

A forty-three-year-old woman was always, and in just about any social situation, trying to manipulate the conversation so that she could receive praise and approval. Her need for attention, therefore, was paramount. She needed to be central and wished for her desires to be always quickly (instantly) gratified.

Along with such typical hysteric features, she had an exceedingly strong need to rely on her appearance to attract people, and would utilize dramatic displays in her conversation with others as well as try to depend on any kind of sexual and seductive suggestion (toward men) that might successfully achieve her goal. Her goal was to be paid attention to, and of course loved.

With respect to the issue of suggestion, this woman was highly suggestible. Her bold social dramatic presentation was a cover for a more truly underlying dependent attitude. In her dependent truer personality, she felt undereducated and not very well aware of events in the world around her, and she used her husband as her main repository source for information. Because of her personal concerns, she found it difficult to focus on the objective material one learns in school, and in fact, barely made it out of high school.

When asked about her school experience, she remembered that in class, she was always preoccupied with personal concerns about how she looked, which of the boys liked her, and generally whether her friends would be true to her or rather were just fair-weather friends. Thus, she was always insecure and her tension about such insecurity made it necessary for her to try to latch onto any suggestion that people made about what was going on, or about things to do. Because of her insecurity, over the years she habitually became highly suggestible as well as agreeable to the demands of others, and this kind of behavior also revealed a pervasive dependent orientation.

She needed to conquer, and this accounted for her highly seductive behavior. Such conquest needs are usually attributed to oedipal strivings with respect to competition with the same-gender parent. In this woman's case, such an understanding seemed to correspond with her history insofar as throughout her childhood she was apparently in competition with her sister and mother as to who was the prettiest—and in a blatant oedipal display, the real concern was who daddy felt was the prettiest.

She would try to display her physical appearance to what she considered to be its best advantage—and this was a sexually seductive type of presentation. When this seemed to be working for her she could be tilted toward love and romance by the slightest positive feedback. Her critical judgment would be suspended as a result of the praise and attention she got—in essence, because of the delight she took in being in the spotlight. She would replay how happy it made her to be "washed over" with pleasure.

It was this sort of romantic theme that also characterized most of her fantasy life in which her wishes were just about always being gratified. In contrast, because of her great need for attention, when such focus on her was not forthcoming she would become irritable, impatient, and even angry. This impatience was the key to understanding that she had a low level of frustration tolerance, which is considered a measure of immature development. In addition, her fantasy life of social and sexual conquest contained a grandiosity to it, the purpose of which was to ensure that at least in fantasy, she would be consistently successful in her aims: that is, she would be adequate.

Therefore, it could be seen that for this woman the issue of disappointment was crucial and to be avoided at any cost since disappointment meant that emotion was controlled and static; and therefore this stasis would necessarily mean that she was inadequate and not attractive. In contrast, the need to avoid disappointment meant that her emotional life was free and this certainty that emotion was definitely not controlled contributed mightily to her need for conquest and to her sense of assurance that such conquest was possible; that she could be flamboyant, eye-catching, and dazzling.

The More Normally Inclined Histrionic Style

In the more moderate form of a hysterical disposition, the release of emotion as a way to minimize anxiety takes the form of behavior characterized by a socially flamboyant style (although not one that is garishly over-the-top), as well as a sense of mastery in social or interpersonal situations. Therefore, this more moderate histrionic style is seen as one wherein the person expresses entitlements but not the over-entitlement of the classic histrionic personality.

Therefore, even though emotion is needed to be released in this sort of person in order for such a person to feel balanced and free of discomfort, nevertheless when the histrionic type is in fact a more moderate one, then judgment can be consistently rather good, magical wishes and strong dependency feelings need not be in the absolute ascendancy, and the need for immediate gratification (although a rather pressing need) is not necessarily governing all behavior all of the time. It is true that even in the moderate histrionic personality the individual is still strongly affected emotionally by momentary conditions, yet these existential and fleeting intrusions do not necessarily become destabilizing. Since wishes are not particularly and intensely inundating such a person, then it is easy to see that passivity (as a function of the absence of a romantic encounter) as a usual behavioral stance of the histrionic type does not in the more moderate type dominate the person's wish system or behavior as nearly as it does for the more severely affected histrionic type.

Because of better functioning and a more mature approach to life, these moderate histrionic types can in fact be quite interesting in intimate relationships because they do not only see and do solely what they want to see and do. In this sense the use of the defense mechanism of denial is implemented much less frequently. In contrast, in the conventionally demonstrated or highly activated histrionic type, a great deal of selective perception is seen (you see only what you want or need to see) and a great deal of perceptual defense is utilized (you screen out everything you don't want to see). In the more moderate histrionic type, these denial-and-compensatory mechanisms might actually, in fact be seen but only with lower voltage.

The only remaining similarity, in the high-versus-low-activated histrionic types, would be issues of the need for a good deal of external stimulation, a rather dramatic expression of feelings, a greater repertoire of romantic fantasy, and a preference not to be isolated or alone. In the more severe type, the romantic need creates an endless string of serial relationships and potential relationships. The more moderate type invites more stable, and certainly fewer, relationships.

CHAPTER TEN

The Narcissistic Style

THIS PERSON BEHAVES with a sense of entitlement that belies an underlying feeling of inadequacy and uncertainty. The sense of entitlement fuels a fantasy life that is entirely compensatory (ego-enhancing because of a dread of obscurity), and characterized by the person's imagined heroic deeds, as well as the needed adulation from a host of similarly imagined acolytes. As such, this person's drive for aggrandizement is intense, and is accompanied by a relentless need of grandiose wishes—fantasies of fame, wealth, notoriety, and even nobility.

In life, this person is most happy when in response to admiration from others such admiration is actually achieved. Correspondingly, in fantasy, achievement deeds are overvalued and daydreams contain themes of power, success, and conquest. Further, in actual functioning in life this person will exaggerate all successes as if even any minor successful achievement qualifies as the greatest of achievements. In other words, all positive achievements and attributes are for purposes of display, maximized.

Consistent with a need to be singularly wonderful, such a person also focuses on brilliance and beauty, both with respect to personal aesthetic sensibility as well to the certainty that such qualities assumedly apply to the self and would be valued by others. In addition, and as might be predicted, such a person believes the self to be unique and will do anything to be envied. Correspondingly such a person will try to associate with others who have already gained notoriety and are considered to be luminaries in whatever field. It is a formula that equates another's greatness as though it automatically translates to one's own greatness. Correlated to this need to be seen as important and unique, is this person's inclination to be exhibitionistic.

Personality characteristics of haughtiness and even arrogance accompany this person's desire to maintain a stance of superiority. To support this sort of need for superiority, such a person is also almost completely opportunistic. In this opportunistic quest for conquest and triumph, such a person neglects to sufficiently develop the altruistic quality of empathy—feeling for others. Whenever any empathetic or philanthropic impulse does indeed get expressed, it is usually with great homage and deference, and as such contains the characteristic of nobility—and then to others does indeed seem noble. Yet, in its underlying motive, this kind of generous impulse will be impelled by a basic sense of superiority granted by its grand gesture. The main point here is that such acts of generosity, humility, modesty, or homage, are basically informed, and in the service of the narcissistic need of adoration from others. In addition, such characteristics are based upon the person's swoon regarding a strong confirming need of self-esteem, and in the service of the comfort and gratification of self-love.

With respect to the deleterious effects of such a search for narcissistic gratification, such a person is characteristically super-sensitive to criticism, and consequently will be similarly super-sensitive even to minor slights. Self-doubt and a sense of feeling undervalued accompany these sensitivities. As such, a person who is identified to be one displaying a Narcissistic Personality Style will be easily subject to feeling shamed, and the response to this feeling of shame will be, consequently, to feel angry.

Along with this vulnerability to the random indifference of the world that any individual experiences, the narcissistic type will be constantly comparing the self to others, and then trying to manage feelings of envy in an endless attempt to quell feelings of inferiority. Thus, the sense of security that is gained from an elevated sense of self is largely hoped for, and can be actually accrued by compliments and favorable responses from others. This is especially gratifying when such a person is treated by others as unique and quite special—either as highly intelligent, creative, or, of course, attractive. When real adoration is absent however, this kind of person will then attempt to manipulate others in an urgent quest for recognition. In the absence of this kind of adoring feedback, the narcissistic person will then rely largely on fantasy wishes containing grandiose fantasy scenarios in which naturally, the self is adored.

Of course, in order to achieve the narcissistic (self-love) gratification in fantasy (no less in reality) this person will usually exaggerate the extent of personal talents and abilities so that they appear to be quite extraordinary. In reality, these personal qualities are usually not exceptional largely because such a person was typically always too occupied with aggrandizement to be focused (in the sense of real functioning) on solid achievement. Thus, because of this misguided and misdirected amount of psychic energy that was invested in fantasy and manipulation, such a person usually ends up as underachieved, and in most cases, profoundly underachieved.

Finally, because of this misguided and misdirected energy that was invested in fantasy and manipulation, this person needs to keep emotion from being controlled so that an abundance of activity keeps the personal inner life from being examined. By avoiding an analysis of one's inner life, the narcissistic person then avoids experiencing any inferiority feelings. For this kind of personality, the linchpin to avoiding anxiety, is for sure, to keep emotion from being controlled. Therefore, keeping emotion free is the consistent aim here.

Case Examples

Case 1: The Narcissistic Personality – A Symptom Sketch

This woman who was sixty-four-years old, had never married, and had developed behavior that would frequently antagonize others. She was constantly trying to be the center of attention and because of it could easily lose sight of proper social comportment. For example, when she joined some of her friends on vacation, she would insist on choosing the hotel, then she would insist on choosing the bed near the window, and often, she would even insist on sitting at the dinner table in the center of things.

She was a former teacher in the public-school system of a large city where she demonstrated similar traits of entitlement. In this, her worklife, she was occasionally accused of fabricating stories that made someone else look bad while giving to herself the rationale of maturity and correctness. In this sense, this woman would do almost anything for the gaining of an appreciable ascendancy in relationships, as well as behaving in a way that contained an even impatient wish for attention.

Because she was also a diligent and conscientious teacher, she spent inordinate amounts of time preparing materials for her students, beautifying the classroom with an assortment of decorations and student work, and along with this she gradually became justifiably recognized for her efforts. For this, she was finally recognized with a Teacher-of-the-Year acknowledgment—an award she confessed harboring in her wishes for a decade. According to others around her, it was actually an award well deserved.

On another positive note, she was quite a productive person, and in her spare time sang in a choir. Thus, this woman had many stellar qualities. The problem was her narcissism—a narcissism that on the negative side made it difficult for people on a personal basis to like her, and on the positive side, enabled her to work at an inordinately high capacity despite the fact that it was motivated by her desire for recognition.

What she did with the Teacher-of-the-Year Award was quite interesting in view of her diagnosis, which contained this glaring narcissistic component. She duplicated the certificate and framed it so that one copy hung conspicuously in her classroom, another copy was hung in her apartment, and a third copy was neatly folded and always carried in her handbag. It is one thing to carry something one loves in a handbag, knowing it is there, but it is another thing to carry such a prize in one's handbag, and here and there, show it to those you meet.

Case 2: The Narcissistic Personality

A forty-five-year old unmarried man was seemingly misdiagnosed as a manic-depressive personality largely because he would have definite mood swings. He was a university professor who would sometimes be moody and at other times somewhat euphoric, and this kind of variability in his personality led psychiatrists to feel that he was both a manic and a depressive personality—currently described essentially, as bipolar.

The truer diagnosis of this person was that of narcissistic personality in which it was both easy for him to become self-idealized, wherein he would revel in what he considered to be great personal achievement or recognition, or when feeling criticized or for a time remaining unrecognized, he could also easily begin to devalue himself. In the state of devaluation, he would appear to be depressed although, really, he was in the thrall of disappointment.

Hence, his so-called manic diagnosis was actually a self-proclaimed greatness that gave him reason to feel euphoric and valued, while his depressive diagnosis (within the manic/depressed diagnostic sense) was actually his morbid sense of feeling devalued (his disappointment). It is this sense of an over-idealized self as well as a devalued sense of self that comprises this variable shift in mood. It may resemble a manic and depressive shift, but it is rather a classic dynamic of a narcissistic personality. That is, that when the person's exaggerated sense of entitlement is not met, and even rather thwarted, this will consistently lead to feelings of despondency (appearing to be depression), and the despondency will consist of components of anger, shame, and even humiliation.

In this man's quest for continued self-idealization, he was always focused on what he could derive from any situation so that his relationships were shallow and based upon his primary concern solely with himself along with a true absence of concern for anyone else. In addition, he was quite fragile with respect to feeling the slightest criticism, and this sort of response from another person could send him into a humiliating tailspin. With respect to his students there was always his tension with regard to how they would evaluate him. And even if one or two evaluations weren't good, or good enough, he would be hurt.

Thus, here was a person who sought the power of superiority and so rather than considering his work to be valued for itself, he always thought about his work in terms of the prestige such achievement could or would bestow. In this sense, he was also always expecting good things to happen to him because of "who he was." The question of who he was would be answered in a way that only he was privy to. Yet he actually believed, expected, and felt that others should realize his self-endowed special entitlements. Of course when such recognition was not forthcoming (based solely on his thinking that the world should already know how great he was), he would become disappointed.

This man's narcissism reflected classic features summarized by a somewhat exhibitionistic aggrandizing need for constant attention and verbalized admiration from others. The greatest hope of his shared time was his worst fear of self-devaluation, which in the extreme would make him feel empty and worthless.

The More Normally Inclined Narcissistic Style

In a narcissistically inclined person—one who is not classically narcissistic—the wish for entitlement exists but a demanding insistence on entitlement is absent. In addition, when entitlement wishes are thwarted the more normally inclined narcissist will of course be very disappointed but not undone by the disappointment. In such a person, a stronger ego not only prevents dispiritedness based upon any blow to self-esteem but rather, although not loving it, accepts "the demotion" with a greater sense of balance. Nevertheless, the search for approval and success is quite prominent in such a person, and to be admired is certainly highly valued. This is to say that the wish for adoration commonly seen in the classic narcissistic personality is replaced in the more normally inclined narcissist with wished-for hopes for simply received admiration or even simple appreciation.

Usually such a person will in all likelihood establish ways and means to achieve something important and thereby will experience the recognition so very much valued. In fact, a usual strategy developed in the more normally inclined narcissist can include devoting time on projects that can be done in a rather anonymous fashion so that potential criticism is avoided but ultimate kudos can be achieved for whatever is the accomplishment of the project. It is almost as if by engaging in something that is rather anonymous, this type of person becomes the one who, in the process, adores the self.

Thus, the more normally inclined narcissist is eager for the visibility of talent and intelligence, and the feedback thereof, but is secure enough to resist any obvious exaggeration of such talent and/or intelligent displays of self. Yes, daydreams of power and recognition do exist in such a person, but these are not of a magnitude, intensity, or depth of purpose that would completely swallow the person's attention, time, and energy.

The most evident characteristic of the narcissistic picture that frequently does emerge in such a person concerns a quality of impatience. It is an impatience that has a petulant and even arrogant cast to it. Yet, such a person is also frequently empathetic (even noble), and is able to restrain anger based upon experienced slights. Extreme opportunistic impulses and a potential picture of insistent visible superiority also seem absent in such a more normally inclined narcissist as compared to the classic narcissist.

Finally, such a more-normally inclined narcissistic person can struggle with underlying narcissistic needs but will also require (hope for) loving reciprocity and consistent fairness with a relationship partner.

CHAPTER ELEVEN

The Psychopathic Style (Antisocial)

THE CHARACTERISTIC STYLE of this psychopathic or antiso-cial type is a decided lack of concern about the boundaries of other people. As such, frequent boundary violations occur. This means that the psychopathic person does not consider the feelings of others, is only concerned with the need to gain advantage, and is frequently involved in delinquent and unlawful behavior.

This issue of the boundaries of others and their violation deserves a concatenation of synonyms because such links can truly express the core issue in the behavior of such people. These synonyms of boundary violation include *breaching, infringing, transgressing, invading, encroaching, molesting, intruding, assaulting, trampling-on.*

In addition, deceitfulness, lying, cheating, stealing, and pro-miscuity are usual examples of the kind of delinquency seen in behavior of the psychopathic personality.

Other types of psychopathic behavior involve severe spousal abuse, physical fighting, other such violent activities, and even pre-meditative murder. Accompanying personality features include an exploitative orientation toward others, impulsivity (doing impul-sive things without thinking about the consequences), irritability, aggressiveness, poor judgment, and poor planning.

In view of these virulent boundary violations, this sort of per-son does not really care about the safety of others, is entirely irresponsible, and of course, such instability makes it so that the psychopathic type can almost never really be responsible—as in the consistent holding of a job. This rather pitiful picture of instability is also one of superficiality, immaturity, manipulativeness, and most importantly, it shows an absence of conscience.

Whenever there is an insufficiency of conscience in a person, it is always accompanied by a conspicuous absence of guilt or remorse, and in addition reflects an absence in such a person of a normal development of empathy. As such, the psychopathic person who exhibits this Antisocial Style just about never feels such empathy, and therefore also experiences no guilt or remorse with respect to any manipulations, expediencies, or boundary violations toward others. In this respect, it is probably safe to say that such a person has never internalized (taken in, absorbed) a sense of control, or understood the importance of controls or of identification with a kind/decent mentor or parent.

All delinquent behavior is rationalized, and this person remains indifferent to the negative or seriously damaging effects of these delinquent acts on others. The consequences of these antisocial acts also never influence the person in a positive manner, insofar as no learning takes place from negative consequences. This kind of person simply never learns from experience in the sense of doing better. Unfortunately, since it never gets better (which leaves such a person to the fates), it makes others who come into contact with this person quite vulnerable to this individual's antisocial impulses. Such impulses, as mentioned, can be dangerous.

The central need inherent in the Psychopathic Style is to continue to generate endless external stimulation in order for emotion not to be controlled. In theory, if emotion would be controlled, this sort of person could possibly begin to feel a psychological paralysis almost completely due to a terror of the interior life that is presumably quite impoverished. That is to say such a person feels the internal life to be silent and actually, more or less empty, and therefore tries to continue to stimulate the environment in order to provide something alive. This is what is meant by the need to create endless externally exciting conditions.

In addition to a terror of the silent inner life, the other motivation to create such continuous external stimulation is the antisocial person's overall impatience and short attention-span. It is the reflex of acting-out that prevents a feeling of psychological paralysis, and therefore anxiety is managed because emotion is calibrated in such a person to be in a dyscontrolled state—loose. The person, therefore, can be naturally or reflexively impulsive.

It is clear that the psychopathic style is one of pleasure seeking, and as such, dissatisfactions and frustrations are avoided at all costs. In this sense, this kind of person is always on the move because boredom is equivalent to silence and stillness. This is called *a proclivity toward motoric behavior* – the motor is always going. But in order for the motor to be always going, such a person operates with defense mechanisms that facilitate such a pattern. These defenses include a heavy reliance on the repressive mechanism—preventing this person from looking within and contemplating possible problems. In addition, the defense of regression or the inability to control impulse (also seen in children), simultaneously permits immature motoric behavior to be sustained.

Along with this motoric behavior and immaturity, such a person is also reckless, blames others for everything that goes wrong, and as might be expected disregards rules and regulations. Because of an obvious impatience, such a person is also always in a position of underachievement. In other words, such a person can't sit still long enough to accrue expertise in anything.

The need to continue to generate stimulation, as a result of this psychopathic style really reveals the central need to keep emotion from being controlled. As mentioned, in this way emotion is loose and can keep this kind of person from experiencing what is most defended against—a sense of a deadened inner life.

Case Examples

Case 1: The Psychopathic Personality – a Symptom Sketch

An attractive forty-year-old man was functioning with a severe inferiority complex but had it concealed with a persona filled with charm and smooth talking. He always dressed well and was motivated to behave in a way that encouraged people to see him as a substantial person, someone of value and worth. In truth, he felt entirely devious and opportunistic with others, and in psychotherapy consultation could admit never to feeling authentically interested in others.

To his therapist he would boast about whom he fooled and how he gained an advantage in this or that situation. He correctly believed that his therapist would need to keep the information confidential so that he wasn't worried about his reputation being soiled by these revelations to the therapist. It was his greatest pleasure to enjoy recounting these successful exploitative events. The therapist could vividly see the appreciable extent of this man's need to experience a sense of triumph.

Since he had never pursued a career path, then whatever achievements he would obtain were gained in the absence of any real persistent efforts. Therefore, if the dignity one derives is from the pursuit of valuable goals through one's consistent efforts—and usually difficult travails—then this man was without such dignity, and never had the opportunity to experience the building up of normal ego that also develops through the effort that goes into gaining solid achievement.

Thus, his prime psychopathic symptom concerned his typical motive to gain best advantage in any possible situation. In this sense he was always watching and observing any and all situations that would lend themselves to his interventions in order to gain such advantage. Therefore, this kind of sustained scouting qualifies as a form of stalking behavior. In the end it could be said that this man's chief psychopathic symptom was that of stalking in order to take advantage of someone, more or less, actually, of anyone.

Case 2: The Psychopathic Personality

A fifty-three-year-old man had been incarcerated as a juvenile when he was sixteen (for breaking and entering), served time in prison, but managed never again to be caught for any of his ongoing nefarious activities. His typical callousness was in evidence every time he borrowed money and then never paid it back. He was not concerned about it one way or the other despite ardent pleas from people who needed to be repaid. Over the years he would repeat the same irresponsible and deliberate scam on any number of unsuspecting people who apparently were fooled by his charm and loquaciousness.

Since because of his impulsive behavior it was impossible for him to sustain or even gain employment, instead, from time to time he would start up a small retail business, which after a while would unfailingly fail. Nevertheless, he managed to leave each of these enterprises with more money than he had when he entered. But the money didn't last because he demonstrated typical psychopathic lassitude. He invested limited energy into any of his businesses and only relied on the swiftest way to renege on his debts.

He was always on the move and this represented his need to keep the stimulation going and in order to keep his emotions and impulses free from constraints. In this sense, he was a classic emotionally dyscontrolled personality who had a tendency always to blame others for things that weren't going right. His blaming tendency was also his way of keeping his conscience clear and at the same time creating objects toward whom he could be excitedly angry. He was a classic underachiever, quite self-centered, with very little, or any, remorse or guilt or conscience. He was also a lifelong gambler and was promiscuous. He could be described as a typical hedonist. Of course as was the case and as could be predicted, he was never involved in any long-term relationship. In addition, he had a complete disregard for the truth.

All in all, this man lived a life of acting-out manipulative activity with what could be considered the condition of an impoverished inner life. His solution was to create mindless acts in order to animate or keep himself in a continuous state of responsiveness and excitement.

The More Normally Inclined Psychopathic Style

Of course it seems as though it is a euphemism or oxymoron to consider what could be defined as a more-normally inclined psychopathic style. Yet, when a person does in fact develop with a propensity toward psychopathic advantage-taking this doesn't necessarily mean that a full-fledged flowering psychopathic personality has developed. In such a case with only low-level acting-out, a person who engages so usually operates with a strong ability to compartmentalize behavior as well as compartmentalizing the emotional reactions to such behavior. For example, such a person can "borrow" a book or a magazine from the waiting room of a doctor's office, and of course do it furtively, and do it well. Even if caught, this person will not have to pay any penalty and the deed will be permanently closed without consequences.

It is these sorts of acts in which such a person engages that constitute delinquent behaviors, but apparently they are carried out in such a way that penalties are not applied, or not even legally warranted. Cheating on tests in school (and doing it expertly) is another example of seeking advantage without the necessary struggle involved in solid achievement. Even getting caught at it might invite some variant of censure but not a jail term.

This is the kind of person who does understand boundaries and by and large will not violate them except and until a circumstance arises where the boundary can be crossed without anyone noticing. Thus, a normally inclined psychopathic type of person may be tempted to act out any number of low-level inappropriate behaviors but also can utilize caution as well as experience some conflict with respect to possible consequences.

Therefore, such a person sometimes lives on the edge of lawlessness but in a way that also contains fail-safe measures. It is a life of inauthenticity but at the same time such a person can have enough of a life that includes friendships, family, achievements, and so forth. This sort of person also feels guilt and remorse, but over time as the guilt and remorse fade, acting-out of small-time thieveries (as an example) again can reappear.

It is also clear that such a person will never engage in activity considered to be a felony. No violence or major infringements will occur, but sneaky little misdemeanors will certainly intermittently occur. These acting-out events will serve the purpose of keeping emotion reasonably dyscontrolled, the additional purpose of which is for the individual to feel periodic relief of tension. In this sense, such a person takes chances but does not engage in wholesale recklessness, is usually in an intermittent search for external stimulation, but can also be quiet, and in this sense there is an absence of a blanket silence of the inner life. Learning from negative experiences does occur but because over time such learning is likely to fade, an immature and incomplete moral development becomes evident. As a postscript, it is noted that such a person will also live life without easily trusting or really confiding in anyone.

Nevertheless, this so-called more normally inclined psychopathic type can, with finesse (and luck), seem to be leading a rather conventional life although without any wholesome intimacy. Furthermore, even in such a low-flying so-called psychopathically inclined (although more normal type) existence, the level of inauthenticity comes across as a distinct although not debilitating immaturity.

Category 3
Emotion-attached Styles

Emotion-attached Styles are chiefly those in which the person seeks promises of safety and shelter in the caring attachment of caregivers and/or authority figures. In this sense these emotion-attached styles seek agreement, and correspondingly usually try to avoid disagreements with those on whom they depend. Such persons are therefore at ease when the affiliation with the caregiver is free of conflict.

The emotion-attached type of personality manages anxiety and emotion by guarding against independent behavior and thinking, in order to assure an achievement of dependent attachment. This sort of pattern or style of personality can be seen in

1. The Dependent Personality
2. The Passive-Aggressive Personality
3. The Inadequate Personality

CHAPTER TWELVE

The Dependent Style

WITH RESPECT TO motive, the main characteristic style of the dependent person is to maintain a central and all-abiding affiliation with either a protective parent, or some other authority figure who similarly offers safety and security. In this sense, this kind of dependent person always, and without fail, seeks agreement with this care-giving figure. Because of such deference, the dependent personality style is one that craves support, and almost by definition, therefore, is basically submissive. Understandably then, in their relationship, the caregiver is automatically dominant.

In order to ensure successful achievement of attachment with a caregiver, behaviors associated with the Dependent Personality Style are such that independent thinking and decision-making recede in favor of seeking and inviting advice. Along with this eschewing of independent thinking and behavior, the dependent person tends to avoid responsibility, relies on the support person for such decision making, and will do almost anything for approval.

Such a person will always be super-sensitive to criticism, and because of prevailing self-doubt, as well as the need for proof of support from the caregiver, will, in all likelihood, require constant reassurance. This need for constant reassurance creates the picture of such a person as an immature individual whose emotionality and momentum toward autonomy became arrested at an early stage of development.

When considering this emotion-attached profile of a dependent style of relating, it becomes apparent that anxiety is always, for this person, in the process of being assuaged; that is, that anxiety gets cured by the assertion of this particular style of dependency—this emotion-attached style. Correspondingly, the event that would be most terrifying for such a person would involve separation from the caregiver, so that in order to prevent even the hint of separation (and to prevent the dreaded fear of separation anxiety), personality tendencies or traits of cooperation, passivity, and of course, compliance, constitute and comprise the core of the dependent person's motivations.

The psychoanalytic understanding of chronic (long-standing), and intense reliance on dependent inclinations, thinking, and behavior, will always—without fail—generate a great deal of underlying anger. Of course, the dependent person who functions with a singular focus on cooperation and agreement with the dominant partner will almost never feel or experience the anger—even though by definition it is theoretically accepted that the anger does, in fact, unconsciously exist beneath the surface and completely out of the dependent person's awareness. As a matter of fact, the typical Sturm und Drang of adolescence is not solely a function of the sudden onset of puberty with its newly experienced flush and rush of hormones. This typical adolescent stage in which is seen a surge of tension, resistance to authority figures, acting-out behavior, and any and all such chaotic experience, is also a derivative of the anger that has been smoldering and accumulating in the unconscious—nicely repressed throughout childhood; a childhood represented chiefly and naturally by a dependency condition that is a typical side effect of childhood experience. The fact is that children throughout these years depend on their caregivers for just about everything: for sustenance, shelter, knowledge, judgment, decisions, education, and so forth. By the time children reach adolescence, all the anger that had accumulated throughout childhood joins with the turmoil generated by the hormonal action of puberty to create what we all know as the rebellious adolescent—one who is iconoclastic (wants to turn over all convention which in essence means gaining the ascendancy over the parent[s], and giving vent to the anger while feeling satisfied with its expression). It is a way of saying: "I am no longer dependent; I am no longer a child, and I now feel empowered."

However, with the dependent person who is already an adult, the situation is somewhat different. The adult who has successfully kept all anger repressed because of needs for continued dependent relationships will correspondingly continue to display personality features of passivity, compliance, and general immaturity. In this sense, underlying accumulated or smoldering anger remains forever repressed in the unconscious, especially because such a person will need to sustain the dependency condition.

Along with this repressed state, such a person, who does not express a normal sense of entitlement, will instead display an entire repertoire of so-called magical wishes. That is to say, without independent activity, what remains is activity in fantasy. Thus, any initiating behavior and any overall spontaneity becomes restricted, and with respect to the issue of compliance, the dependent person will also do anything to avoid being alone, and especially would become terrified of any possible issue of abandonment.

Thus, to circumvent the possibility of separation from the caregiver, the dependent person avoids feeling terrified or anxious or depressed by utilizing a host of defense mechanisms, the most useful of which is to be constantly compensating for a strong sense of inadequacy, and by consistently reinforcing and fortifying the emotion-attached style.

Case Examples

Case 1: The Dependent Personality – A Symptom Sketch
An eighteen-year-old male left his first semester of college after only several initial weeks of the semester. He reported that everything felt "unfriendly" and "cold." Immediately before he left the campus, it was recommended that he report to the counseling office for a guidance session. He was accompanied to the guidance

session by both of his parents whom he had called so that they could come and get him.

It was further reported that this experience of alienation or tension regarding the new situation (being away from home), was reminiscent of this young man's first day of kindergarten at the age of five. At that point of his first day of kindergarten, his mother described the situation as one in which, as she was about to leave him there, he began to whimper. When she actually started to walk out of the kindergarten classroom, his whimpering turned to sobbing, and then as she stepped out of the door, he became almost hysterical.

Apparently, this young man had a consistent history of such experiences of anxiety related to separation experiences from his parents. It also occurred once when at the age of thirteen he had gotten a part-time job delivering newspapers. At the last moment, he decided not to do it, and for the same reason—overly concerned with being on his own and needing to discharge a defined responsibility. In all three of these situations, this young man felt strong separation fears accompanied by feelings of dread and loneliness.

Since he was an excellent student in high school, and since it was a certainty that he would attend college, this separation anxiety symptom of his with respect to his college attendance only abated when the problem was solved—he would attend college close to home, located in his hometown, and live at home.

Case 2: The Dependent Personality

A twenty-four-year-old woman from an affluent family was all of her life quite over-protected. Apparently, she was never encouraged to be independent and therefore, by default, she always sought safe and secure situations. In her case it wasn't that she could not absolutely leave home. In fact, for the first time, at the age of twenty-four, she decided to take a vacation, all with the intention of finding a husband, one who was already successful enough to care for her. Her objective was to be protected from what she considered to be a predatory and uncaring world.

As luck would have it, on this very first vacation gamble she met a man who was in the diplomatic branch of the government and who was well known. He was almost twenty years her senior, and had already become successful because of a difficult international situation that he helped resolve. Within a short period of time they married and this young woman became the picture of the helpful wife who with great elan conducted the household. She directed servants, a chef, a chauffeur, and several housekeepers in organizing their various duties and in keeping the schedule of events of the house.

It was in this kind of endeavor that this woman shone. It was perfect for her. Her husband apparently adored her, and it was a wonderful opportunity for her to feel safe, secure, and cared for. It appeared that actually she had mastery over her environment. In addition, in the role she played as the wife of this elegant and respected man, she also seemed suited to him because again, it appeared that she was an independent person. It also helped that she was quite beautiful.

Underneath it all however, the truth was that she was completely dependent and, for example, actually frightened about even contradicting someone. She was able to be successful because in order not to antagonize anyone, she was self-effacing, and in her interaction with others, assumed what appeared to be a conspicuously modest attitude but which in reality was a natural inclination to be as democratic as possible in order not to invite controversy. Therefore, this so-called egalitarian stance was really a disguise for what was her reflexive response in assuming an inferior position in any relationship. In her case she had the ability and circumstance to conceal her true feelings.

Thus, the lady-of-the-manor role was the perfect scenario for her because she could then avoid any involvements that would give her the feeling of rejection or disapproval from others, or even worse, reveal to others what she felt was her immaturity regarding her rather ubiquitous fear of the world. In her particular wifely role and station in life, it was unlikely that anyone would try to argue with her, or contradict her, or ever be rude to her.

With dependent personalities, a reliance on magical solutions to problems is sought and in this case her entire situation enabled such solutions to be realized. In addition, such personalities generally reveal poor implementation ability as well as a poor ability to initiate acts. Again in her case however, she was surrounded with help-personnel and given this particular circumstance, the truth was that everything would have kept running efficiently whether she was there or not. And knowing this full well enabled this woman to conduct the household with ease while also enabling her to consistently feel safe, especially because she felt that her true feelings and identity were kept from view—but of course she had no way of knowing that others could indeed see her sense of inadequacy and hidden concerns. These sorts of personal concerns are almost impossible to conceal. Behavior reveals much.

In finding this husband and this circumstance, this woman hit upon a once-in-a- lifetime winning lottery that completely satisfied her need for security, safety, and attachment—the perfect complement for someone who was an emotion-attached dependent personality.

The More Normally Inclined Dependent Style

In the more normally inclined dependent personality, the person may be a dependent one but can also be quite accomplished. For example, a dependent man who was a physician was married to a very dominant woman. He was able to function well in structured situations as in his school experiences that clearly and easily tracked him into college, medical school, internship, and residency programs. In all of these pursuits, he was never at loose ends and just followed the prescriptive template that was offered. One thing led to the next and then again to the next. He did his homework, memorized whatever was required and simply swam with the current. He never took vacations or went places that would have taken him far from home. In a nutshell, this man organized his life in such a way as to avoid any situation that was loosely structured.

In view of his need for security and safety, his deferent attitude, and his cooperative and largely compensatory stance in life, he endeared people to him. It was as though his dependency need was not visible, he was not ever angry or in a protest mood, and issues of abandonment fears or of separation anxiety were similarly not apparent to others. Of course he harbored these tensions, but learned how to keep them in check so that they could not be easily detected.

He married a woman who needed to lead and this was a perfect addendum to his lifelong quest for direction and structure. This woman provided plenty of structure insofar as she needed everything to go her way and he wasn't at all bothered by it. She provided the environment in which his needs for security and safety were assured and he never felt threatened by the slightest hint that she might abandon him.

Luckily she appreciated the opportunity to live in luxury and to have it her way all the time. For him, all of it meant that he would not need to surface what was surely in his unconscious and about which he certainly had no notion: his anger harbored by his repression. In this sense of his at-least ostensible store of repressed anger, he also had a discernible symptom of always needing to nap. This compelling need to nap was seen as his acting-out of a decent amount of hidden anger at his personal sense of a profound limitation with respect to his self-imposed reduced degrees of freedom—meaning his limitation with respect to psychological and emotional independence.

This man had always needed reassurance and he was able to accomplish the satisfaction of this need so that in this case circumstance as well as strategy enabled him to be classified as someone who is a more normally inclined dependent type—especially since he was actually able to accomplish his goals, whereas classically considered dependent types are usually and correspondingly, classic underachievers. In the satisfaction of his emotion-attached style, he was able to manage his anxieties especially well because of his successes in virtually both main areas of his life—in his quite successful pursuit of a career (his professional life), as well as in his personal life (by choosing a dominant partner).

CHAPTER THIRTEEN

The Passive-aggressive Style

THE PASSIVE-AGGRESSIVE STYLE of relating contains a basic complement of three distinct variations: these are the Passive-Aggressive, Passive Style; the Passive-aggressive, Aggressive Style; and, the Passive-aggressive, Dependent Style. This passive-aggressive personality is one in which an emotion-attached manner in such a person does in fact display an acting-out of repressed anger in these three distinct ways. As a matter of fact, the entire passive-aggressive style is designed both to acknowledge the person on whom the dependency rests, and at the same time to express dissatisfaction and anger toward this person. Thus, it could be said that the motive of the passive-aggressive person is to engage in a covert power struggle with the authority figure while maintaining both the need for dependency as well as simultaneously adopting the pose of independence.

This pose of independence is basically only a pose because such a person who is emotionally attached is also fundamentally dependent on the authority figure and needs the presence of that figure for feeling a reduction of tension. Yet, this emotionally attached, passive-aggressive person is one who harbors resentment about this very emotionally attached dependency.

In the acting-out of this resentment, the central motivation of such a personality style is designed to frustrate authority while avoiding punishment. It is a clever design and is organized this way in order to salvage some sense of autonomy (independence) by simultaneously sustaining a sense of defiance. This is done with a kind of perverse pleasure in maintaining affiliation with the other person while at the same time frustrating the other person. It is a defiance ingeniously masked by cooperation. Examples of such perverse joining of objectives include: tardiness, procrastination, forgetting, and not completing tasks. Thus in an inventive, yet immature manner, a person that expresses the emotion-attached style of the passive-aggressive personality can be sullen, argumentative, and show protest behavior, while managing to salvage the dependency position with the authority figure (although of course, with risk).

Case Examples

The variations of this passive-aggressive style include:

Passive-aggressive Personality: Passive Style—Here the person expresses anger through passivity. There is both an implicit and explicit promise to cooperate, but anger is stimulated in the dominant partner by the passive person's behavior of procrastination, incompleteness, withholding, and forgetting.

Case 1:Passive-aggressive Personality –Passive Style
A Symptom Sketch
A forty-eight-year-old homemaker was married to an engineer. They had two daughters who were in their teen years. Theirs was an adequate marriage except that the husband complained bitterly that his wife would always forget to do something when she set the table for dinner. He provided examples of this, which she acknowledged was true. She admitted to never feeling she remembered everything about setting the table, so for example, a napkin or some utensil or salt or pepper or a side dish was invariably forgotten. Apparently, every evening this man heard the same sud-

den surprise from her: "Oh my God, I forgot the asparagus!" Or, he would sit down for dinner and everyone would have a napkin except him. His typical feeling was that she was expressing hostility to him in a very passive, so-called innocent way, and for all intents and purposes, he was obviously right. Of course, her hostility may not have been strictly about him as much as it might have been about needing to stay home all day and do chores about which she felt bored and angry. Whatever the reason, such behavior on her part seemed typically passive-aggressive: passive type.

Passive-aggressive Personality: Aggressive Style—Here, the person expresses anger more directly. Examples of such behavior include overtalkativeness, quarrelsomeness, interruptiveness, argumentativeness, and even physical fighting. Yet, despite this bold and bellicose attitude, the wish for dependency on the authority figure is still a prominent feature in the needs of the personality.

Case 2: Passive-aggressive Personality – Aggressive Style
A Symptom Sketch
A fourteen-year-old boy had a history throughout his childhood of hogging the spotlight from other family members as well as from classmates in school, and generally talking a blue streak. Despite his strong attachment to his father, who was employed as a hospital administrator, this boy needed to act as strong as his father and display obvious bellicose behavior, and yet, was quite normally, and in an overall way attached to his parents (and his father specifically). After engaging in such annoying behavior, he would also typically calm down and then become cooperative. It was an example of a classic passive-aggressive style, aggressive type.

Passive-aggressive Personality: Dependent Style—Here the person expresses anger through behavior that can be considered cloying (or sickening the other person with sweetness). Such a passiveaggresssive-dependent person will volunteer to be ever at the beck and call of the authority figure, but to a suffocating extent.

Case 3: Passive-aggressive Personality –Dependent Style
A Symptom Sketch

A thirty-year-old man was extremely cloying with those he professed to be helping. With his wife he almost jumped into her computer, behaving in a way that was exceedingly sacrificial. He would type all of her graduate-school papers, run to the library to pick up the books she needed, and do various and sundry things that she had not even asked for. In his day job, he worked as an assistant to a college professor (for a minimum wage), and did the same kind of cloying sacrificial behavior there as well. This was all in the service of his dependency needs on both of these people while at the same time he was expressing his hostility unconsciously by driving them crazy with his so-called help. In this respect, this man's behavior is considered classically passive-aggressive with a dependent style.

Case 4: The Passive-aggressive Personality

All in all, in each of these passive-aggressive variations, the aim of the person of this style, to whatever extent successful, is to frustrate the authority figure while trying to avoid punishment—and this in the attempt to remain emotionally attached and dependent. It is in this sort of attachment (less a cohesion with the authority figure and more an adhesion), that in the passive-aggressive style is found a central motive to reduce anxiety by ultimately remaining emotionally attached. Yet, at the same time there is a visible and persistent pattern of actually also needing a hostile separation from the authority figure, basically in the absence of punishment or retaliation from the authority figure. Nevertheless, even though the anger and aggression challenge the attached relationship, these challenges do not usually undo such relationships and ultimately, the gratification of the passivity, the aggression, or hostility, along with the dependency and along with the attachment-need is, at least, partially satisfied.

A classic example of such overall behavior in a typical passive-aggressive mode occurs frequently in restaurants when the waiter takes the order and walks away to fill the order but the patron had forgotten to add something, and then for the longest time tries to attract the waiter's attention, but the waiter does everything not to look in the patron's direction, walks all over the restaurant and serves others, but pays no attention to the frustrated patron.

In such a case the waiter, who was extremely charming at first, is now confronted with the patron complaining about being neglected. It is only then that the waiter will charmingly and seemingly innocently begin to apologize profusely. Thus, the waiter who is passive-aggressive can express his underlying anger by succeeding in making the other person angry, and then apologize so that in all likelihood he will be forgiven. However, in such cases the apology will be underscored with additional passive-aggressive acts. For example the waiter might apologize with sufficient deference and supplication, and at the same time offer his hand in a handshake to indicate that all is okay. The patron will most likely begin to be mollified by such deference and supplication, agree to the handshake only to experience the waiter's wet hand.

This passive-aggressive person thus aims to act out such underlying anger and aggression, and at the same time hopes to retain the attachment—but beware!

The More Normally Inclined Passive-aggressive Style

In the more normally inclined Passive-aggressive Style, power struggles are kept at a lower voltage by only intermittently frustrating the other (and not doing it so consistently or expertly), by eliminating cloying behavior (that would surely sicken the other), and by not appearing to be so dependent (although latent dependency needs still strongly exist). Similarly sacrificial behavior is far less (although still characteristic), and the frustration of the other is not intense enough to worry the passive-aggressive person about ostracism, actual punishment, or even abandonment.

Such a more normally inclined passive-aggressive person can enjoy social interaction and can be a reasonably decent partner in a relationship. Of course, forgetfulness usually will be quite apparent, but the passive-aggressive person will most likely hope that the partner will attribute such forgetfulness to an idiosyncratic personality and therefore will be able to rationalize any anger resulting from it.

Even though because of the nature of passive-aggressive impulses the underlying motive of such a person is to frustrate or anger the partner, nevertheless, in this more benign passive-aggressive person, such impulses are quite unconsciously limited or moderated, and may even be somewhat better consciously controlled. Of course, the passive-aggressive trait cluster of behaviors will still be noticeable.

In addition, the more normally inclined passive-aggressive person usually assumes a position of righteousness and fairness in dealing with the partner (whether actually fair or not) and will characteristically behave righteously or indignantly should any accusation be leveled that implies passive-aggressive motives.

It usually works.

CHAPTER FOURTEEN

The Inadequate Style

THE INADEQUATE PERSONALITY Style is labeled in this manner because the central problem here is in an under-response virtually in every arena of the person's life. In the contemporary psychiatric-classification systems, as a category, this inadequate type has been deleted. Nevertheless, clinicians see such people more than just occasionally. Such individuals under-respond to the complement of intellectual, emotional, and social demands of life. Lassitude, ineptness, lack of stamina, and also less-than-uniformly good judgment, become evident in this person's functioning, although in some cases this sort of problem is not necessarily nor immediately reflected in results of some IQ tests.

Thus, such a person can be quite able to navigate through life in a way that continues to produce a typical under-response. Although it is frequently seen that results on IQ tests are sometimes not significantly affected by such under-response, there are other tests that do identify the problem indeed with lowered IQ scores. When personality functioning does affect IQ, it is in the area of motor behavior—that is, when required to perform or to use one's hands to manipulate objects the person's typical lassitude affects performance. In such cases, there will be a discrepancy between those IQ tasks on tests that simply require verbal answers in contrast to much lower scores on test items that require one "to motorically" manipulate items. The sense of inertly sitting and answering questions suits such a person better than when this person is required, so to speak, to get up and go.

It becomes obvious that such a person manages tension and anxiety through the style of remaining emotionally attached to a primary caregiver as well as by behaving in a manner that requires support from this primary caregiver. In addition, this person's under-response occurs in the arenas of relationships generally, in sex specifically, in school, and in jobs. It is the case however, that such individuals, usually at some point in their employment history, lose jobs, and then inevitably, become essentially unemployable.

By and large, such an inadequate personality style is one in which the person functions with an obvious inferiority feeling, in which performance is constricted, and even any trace of self-assurance is, of course, almost entirely erased. In order to salvage some self-esteem, such a person will exaggerate the importance of any given interactional or interpersonal situation—so that a melodramatic sentimentality is frequently seen in the person's response to various situations. This exaggerated so-called response-of-importance invites such a person to feel as though involved in significant matters, but then also proves to contribute to less than good judgment with respect to varieties of experiences.

In this sense of exhibiting poor judgment, it is the primary caregiver who is called upon to rescue this person from all sorts of self-defeating circumstances. These self-defeating circumstances leave such a person with an ever-increasing sense of risk-aversion—so much so that an increase in the tendency toward dependency, passivity, and withdrawal begin (together, as a cluster of traits), to act as major-personality signature that becomes characteristic of the person's emotional profile. In short, such a person is then seen primarily as one who gains a sense of safety by fortifying and further reinforcing an emotion-attached personality style in which needs for dependency and attachment are basic orientations that the person uses to navigate life.

Similar to a classically dependent-personality style, this inadequate personality has the emotion of anger under complete control. Thus, in the absence of any show of anger, this person comes across with a smooth exterior—especially when behavior is not an issue; that is, in talking to such a person, it may be difficult to predict the inadequacy of functioning. This is so because verbal ability will usually be adequate—even good.

As evidence of the inadequacy of functioning of this kind of person, it is pretty clear that a prediction of underachievement usually would be accurate. For example, the inadequate personality style is one that needs step-by-step instruction for any function to be undertaken successfully, and then would benefit from ongoing supervision in order to sustain whatever achievement has already been accomplished.

The particular defenses that comprise an emotional-security platform for this kind of person include a regressive immature tendency that assures an emotionally attached style (in order to invite care), and also serves this particular style by assuring shallow, immature, and fumbling behavior. In addition, the defensive mechanism of compensating for inferiority feelings enables this person to treat situations with an air of importance (melodramatic sentimentality) which is, of course, essentially inappropriate. Further, such a person utilizes excessive rationalization to try to massage and distract oneself from such inappropriateness.

All in all, it is the across-the-board under-response that characterizes such a person, making it absolutely necessary for this kind of person to be emotionally attached to a primary caregiver or authority figure, thereby successfully nullifying any anxiety about functioning in life. This is essentially how such a person manages tension and anxiety.

Case Examples

Case 1: Inadequate Personality – A Symptom Sketch

A twenty-eight-year-old man was unemployed because on his job and at the end of the workday he continued to leave work unfinished. He was sorting mail in a large company, and although bright, he couldn't quite ever finish the quota of work required of him. And this inability to reach his goals became typical for him.

Finally, he was fired from his job. Since over the past several years this was the fifth or sixth job failure, he and his wife decided that she would be the breadwinner while he kept house. This was a perfect solution for him because then he could take his time throughout the day so that the tasks required to keep the house in order could, in fact, possibly be completed. Yet, here too, he couldn't quite organize his time or his energies to do whatever it took to do the job in a way that would offer him a decent closure experience.

His typical grade at former jobs would probably at best be a C minus. At home in his new task to keep the house in order, he did better, but still not a grade "A." His relationship with his wife did not suffer, however. Since they were kids, she had always been attracted to him, and in addition, she herself didn't really care very much about how the house was kept. Since they had no children nor planned for children, then she was quite happy to have landed him and was even happy about his attachment and dependency on her.

This was a clear case of repetitive job-loss as a symptom of an inadequate personality style in a person who was essentially a perfect example of an emotionally attached type.

Case 2: The Inadequate Personality

A sixty-year-old man who was twice divorced had two sons and found himself estranged from both. In addition, he had a history of underachievement and under-response to the various jobs that he held, but at the age of fifty finally found a menial job in a hanger factory where clothing hangers were both manufactured and exported. His job was mostly to count. He counted packages and noted their contents, and he counted packages going to specific clients. The main point was that the president of the company had known his family so that luckily his performance didn't depend on any particular quota of packages to be counted or sorted. In addition, the president of the company apparently liked him, so that his job was secure and he had now kept it for a decade.

If not for these fortuitous circumstances, this man could never have maintained this job. It was his experience in life that almost nothing ever worked out for him. In school he continuously got grades with addenda attached on his report cards indicating that he was bright but below par in his work, or that a check mark would be placed next to the choice: "Could do better," or, "Unsatisfactory work." Other choices on his report card listed: Is doing well; Is doing very well; Excellent work. He was never blessed with any of these.

Each of his sons, at different times, felt exasperated with what they experienced as his neglect but which in reality was his inability to get it together to remember birthdays, or have the energy to organize himself to purchase gifts, or to respond appropriately with respect to the issue of "doing" in any number of other ways. Gradually, their relationship to him became iffy, and at some point their contact with him was only occasional.

Therefore, this man's only pleasure was in his job. He was entirely engrossed in the satisfaction he got from the security of being liked by the president of the company and took solace in the fact that he could handle the job the way he wanted to. Thus, his inadequate personality style met its corresponding environmental situation that didn't undo him, and this enabled him to sustain a vital emotional attachment. It was his only decent relationship. Otherwise, he lived a rather secluded life.

The More Normally Inclined Inadequate Style

It is clear that there are better or higher-functioning people who nevertheless can be categorized as inadequate types. In many such cases, the person has better-than-average IQ scores, and may even have savant-like abilities. For example, a man of thirty-five was unable to keep a job but was lucky to have found a woman who had a career. He did the housework while each day she went to her job as an accountant. He was a very intelligent person and was particularly good at crossword puzzles. His vocabulary and general fund of knowledge was also very well developed. This was especially interesting because in school he could learn all of his required material but had great difficulty in taking and doing well on exams. On his own with no demands from others he could function quite well. However when a demand from another person was clear, he would falter and was the reason he could not really hold a job or even take an exam.

On his own, therefore, there was no lassitude or ineptness in sight and he would not be generally under-responsive. His problem was always in working with others. With his wife he had what he needed; that is, she wanted him there and so he had his attachment need gratified as well as feeling her support.

In such situations, an inadequate personality type can feel more normal and can actually function better. The consistent loss of jobs, inferiority feelings, and poor judgment do not quite reach the threshold when such a person feels accepted and is not placed in circumstances where many requirements stare him or her in the face. Again, in such circumstances where attachment needs are satisfied, this emotion-attached person will in all likelihood have all of his anger in control.

The melodramatic displays that generate compensatory and even grandiose feelings in such a person, the purpose of which is to obscure inferiority feelings, are absent when attachment to another is secure, and especially when the job situation is not a problem. Under such conditions that favor this inadequate type, a more normally inclined functioning may be seen although this kind of equilibrium will obtain when others are reasonably patient.

•   •   •

Category 4
Emotion-detached Styles

Emotion-detached Styles are those in which the person, in an attempt to manage tension and anxiety, keeps the self from being too influenced by any other person. Thus the mantra with such personality types is: no entanglements. As such, a primary need of such individuals with this emotion-detached style is to remain relatively socially isolated. In this way, emotional security is gained from the social isolation. Such types of personality differ from the schizoid personality of the emotion-controlled group insofar as emotion-detached types are also highly sensitive (wired), feel vulnerable (fragile), and are usually and to some extent, withdrawn (highly self-absorbed).

The emotion-detached personality types include:

1. The Borderline Personality
2. The Depressed Personality
3. The Avoidant Personality

CHAPTER FIFTEEN

The Borderline Style

D UE TO A serious emotional instability, this particular personality style is designed to minimize personality disorganization and the distress of emotion generally by remaining reasonably detached from any even remote possibility of a consistently ongoing and engaging relationship. It is not as if such a person completely ignores relationships as much as it is that such a person finds that in any relationship, the ups and downs are too much to handle, the fine line between feeling very angry or simply tolerating simple frustrations is too fine a line, and the incessant idol worship (idealization) of the same person who is usually also serially disrespected (devaluation), becomes too confusing to think about or to reconcile. Therefore, "it's probably better to keep away for a while" is the inherent philosophical and psychological orientation of such a person. As such, the need for consistency in the cementing and conducting of any serious or important relationship becomes the core problem for such a person, and it is this profound inability to be consistent, and in a stable way related, that is restive at the bottom of it all.

Thus, relationships are limited for such a person, and this reduced repertoire of relationships, in turn, and to some extent, reduces or controls such a person's worst fear. This terrible fear (as well as inescapable anticipation that such borderline individuals typically experience) concerns the issue of a worry about abandonment coexisting with a personal identity-cluster of unstable elements. This unstable sense of self also carries with it a number of potentially deleterious effects of impulses that are, in fact, usually acted-out by most borderline individuals but certainly not by all and with certain of these acts, but again not by all. These are self-damaging impulses including sexually promiscuous and dangerous behavior, use of drugs, overall recklessness, suicidal thoughts and gestures, as well as acts of self-mutilation (localized cutting—usually arms and/or legs). In addition, the borderline style of experience is mostly characterized by the swing of moods in which impulsive behavior is also characteristic along with the main borderline-personality signature of reflexive anger, flare-ups of anger, and paper-thin ability (an inability) to tolerate frustration. Such a person can interrupt any sort of social gathering (even including events that require decorum and special respectfulness). In the middle of such an event, this person can erupt with vocal irritability and predictably toward some important person at the event. Most often when such an eruption occurs, it will invariably cast a pall on the event.

As might be expected, the interior life of the borderline becomes pervaded with bouts of anger or anxiety and/or depressive mood, and these can be followed by a sense of "nothingness," and in the aftermath of some sudden inappropriate social outburst, can also be followed by a sense of terrible regret.

Along with such oscillating moods, temper tantrums can be seen, as well as dissociative reactions such as long periods of time spent in fantasy, and even periods of loss of a sense of personal identity. Occasional paranoid-criticality and suspiciousness is also present, in which the borderline person finds everything to criticize and in turn becomes fully suspicious of the motives of others.

This kind of instability is not intended to denote that the borderline personality is one that straddles neurosis and psychosis. Rather, such instability relates to an absence of sufficient consistency virtually in all areas of the person's life. These include family relationships, general interpersonal relationships, academic functioning, vocational success, and the accruing of consistent personal pleasures that would be considered by most people to be normal and typical pleasures. These normal pleasures can include reading, dinners with friends, attendance at religious ceremonies, TV watching, hobbies, and so forth—all indicating that an average or relatively well-adjusted person can probably engage in these normal pleasures in an habitual or reasonably consistent manner.

A so-called Triad of Conditions expresses the central disorganization in the borderline personality. This Triad of Conditions means that there are three broad areas of disturbance in the borderline type: pan-anxiety; pan-sexuality; and, pan-defensiveness. The reference to the term *pan,* simply means that the problem with anxiety, sexuality, and defensiveness completely affects or permeates all aspects of this kind of person's life. In other words, with respect to this Triad, there is no conflict-free sphere in this person's life regarding anxiety, sexuality, and defensiveness.

Thus, with respect to anxiety, such anxiety is just about ever-present. With respect to the defense system of the personality, this person's defensive structure is ever-shifting. Because of this ever-shiftingness, such a person utilizes a host of defenses usually relevant to, and typically seen in other personality types such as obsessional, hysteric, depressive, and paranoid styles. The sexual factor in the borderline personality can be expressed as essentially immature and experienced as confusing and otherwise polymorphous perverse (sexuality that can be indiscriminate and that obeys no particular or usual expectations).

Therefore in general, because of such instability in all aspects of life, the borderline individual is considered to be an emotion-detached type; that is, the challenge of keeping the emotions cohered, consistent, and controlled cannot at all be easily met. The best bet, then, is that in order to minimize emotional disorganization, such a person attempts to keep oneself emotionally detached—and yet surprisingly fails in this attempt because of the continual secret wish to be involved in everyday life.

Case Examples

Case 1: Borderline Personality – A Symptom Sketch

A twenty-two-year-old woman was a student in an acting school. After only two sessions the instructor asked her to leave the class because she was either blurting out comments, or in a childlike manner expressing displeasure by seeming sullen or, even in her facial expression, displaying an exaggerated and impetuous dissatisfaction. She cried when someone disagreed with something she said. The instructor advised her to see a psychotherapist, which she did.

In therapy sessions her behavior was precisely as had been described in the acting class. She was impulsive along with shifting moods, and she was primarily a tinder-box of anger, and it was these sudden flare-ups of anger that characterized her main borderline condition.

In this young woman's life, one of the problems was that she frequently could not suppress or control her feelings—especially angry feelings. It was almost as if the ability to utilize conscious suppression or reflexive repression was entirely absent. Whatever was on her mind was, in a millisecond, on her tongue. Therefore, she had almost no will or ability to attenuate any angry feeling, and in this sense the urgent and impatient blurting out of things was, of course, highly socially undesirable.

To be emotionally detached, therefore, enabled this young woman's instability to be somewhat less visible and because general social interaction was reduced, the probability of displaying any instability was correspondingly also reduced. Therefore, for this woman such was a clear example of how an emotionally detached person can be self-protective by simply remaining more socially isolated—all in the service of achieving greater emotional security. Yet, in her case the emotional detatchment was only moderately achieved.

Case 2: The Borderline Personality

A severe case of a borderline personality that included a woman's Triad of Conditions (pan-anxiety, pan-sexuality, pan-defensive-ness), was instantly revealed to the staff of a state mental hospital when she was admitted as a patient who could not stop crying.

This was a thirty-five-year-old single woman who only had had sexual experience with one man: Her father had molested her sexually starting at the age of eight and continuing intermittently until she was fifteen, at which time she told him if he didn't stop doing what he was doing she was going to tell her mother. Apparently at that point her father actually ceased molesting her. Three years later this woman left home without announcing it to anyone. The definition of pan-sexuality was satisfied here because of the duration of her molestation despite the fact that it was foisted upon her.

She was a very well mannered woman who had lived alone from the time she departed from her family home at eighteen—exactly when she graduated from high school. It was then that she described finally being able to gather herself together in order to escape what she had come to believe was her sordid life. And she had kept her "secret" to a fault from everyone including her two brothers, her mother, and all of her school friends. When she left home, she never told anyone where she went and it was only seven years later, when she turned twenty-five, that she contacted one of her brothers and eventually told him what had been happening to her all of those years ago.

She had been reared in a Midwest state, and when she fled, she took a bus to New York City. It was in Manhattan that she immediately found a day job as a dishwasher in a luncheonette, and in the evenings also worked as a maid in a hotel. She spent the seven years till she was twenty-five working at both jobs, and living at the Y. During this time she hardly made any friends and, more or less, kept to herself. Miraculously, she was consistently able to go to work each day and to conceal her considerable anxiety and crying episodes. Her considerable tension also qualified as an example of a pan-anxiety. Because she was able to conceal her super-sensitivity which led to her crying, and similarly, was also able to almost completely conceal her flash-angers, and in addition, was able to be consistently employed, her diagnosis, although of the borderline variety nevertheless seems most characteristic of what is clinically considered to be of high-functioning borderline-personality organization.

In addition, she was so sexually traumatized by her father that she became celibate and even though she was also consistently approached by men, each time that such an approach would occur it would send her into an emotional tailspin in which her crying could last for hours. She was also "a cutter," and she would cut herself with a razor blade on the inside of her thighs so that no one could see the damage she was doing. She claimed that whenever she cut herself, it relieved her of unbearable tension. This cutting behavior, as previously cited, is also diagnostically characteristic of a classic borderline personality symptom.

Again, in addition, this woman had an entire plethora of defenses—a pan-defensiveness that ranged from moments of extreme control over herself, as in when, in order to control tension, she would ruminate numbers and perform counting rituals obsessively; or at other times, when she would shift into crying jags that revealed a deep depressive condition. She also experienced moments where she became rather hysterical and the hysteria frequently contained paranoid ideas. Because of this array of symptoms, she was careful to isolate herself from others as much as possible so that when she felt isolated, she also felt safe. She admitted herself to a hospital because one night she literally could not stop crying and began to have violent fantasies about her father. When this had previously occurred she would cut herself, but at this particular evening the cutting did not seem to relieve her of the tension she was feeling, and that gave her a sense that something was different. She cut several times more than usual, became frightened, and called the hospital. Hospital personnel asked her to come in and talk, and that's how the process of her hospitalization began.

In this case, this woman's string of symptoms and defenses, as well as her pervasive anxiety ultimately led to her hospitalization. Her sense of herself was very fragile and yet she was strong enough to leave home, remain on her own for a number of years, and hold two jobs. This was unusual for this type of borderline person since typically with such a condition jobs would be difficult to sustain. In her case, the fact that she was probably a high-functioning borderline type, and the fact that she held onto both jobs, enabled her to remain rather isolated from others in the sense that apparently the kind of jobs they were gave her the freedom to keep any personal relationship on a rather shallow level. She claimed that even on the maid's job (at a low-end hotel) she went to work and went home without ever truly interfacing with coworkers in any significant or personal way. She also described her relief when dining alone and sought to avoid any potential invitations from coworkers to join them for lunch or supper.

Her traumatic condition made her seek isolation and with this isolation and emotional detachment she was somehow able to realize some peace of mind and emotional relief of tension— notwithstanding her cutting and crying episodes. Her main emotional objective was to reduce emotional stimulation. In this way, she had a specific insight into her behavior and knew that she would become too emotionally disorganized with an abundance of external stimulation. Parenthetical social interaction with co-workers sufficed as tacit social interaction.

A More Normally Inclined Borderline Style

It is in the sense of considering what is known as a high-functioning borderline personality that this kind of style can be assessed as "more normally inclined." As a matter of interest, it is quite possible to find such individuals in rather high or important professional positions. They are able to accomplish such a feat because they can feign interest in others while never really fulfilling the assumption of friendship, despite an ability to appear to socialize and to seem to have intimate interactions.

As such, this type of high-functioning borderline person can withstand pressures in the workplace but still, in all, must by all means remain internally aloof and reasonably detached while seeming to be socially available. With such conditions satisfied, this sort of person might only be involved in occasional self-mutilation (cutting behavior), and will only infrequently display strong impulses about devaluing others (which is a trademark of the true borderline personality). In addition, this sort of person will consciously experience the need to be loved in the face of the contrasting need for detachment.

In a word, the more normally inclined borderline type will appear more stable, and although a fundamental unstable sense of self will in most cases exist, nevertheless such a feeling is not as pronounced as it is in the more severe or classic borderline condition. In addition, such individuals are not usually involved in heavy drug use (but will seek psychotropic medication), are not usually reckless (as is typically the case in the borderline profile), and may not engage in tempting suicidal rumination (a characteristic of the classic borderline).

Mood swings may exist but are concealed in a much more effective manner. Although angry impulses needing to burst forth do exist, they can sometimes be quickly diluted by feelings even of anticipated regret. Furthermore, if in fact there is a loss of anger, it is not of the usual catastrophic kind.

Finally, the more normally inclined borderline person although showing similar tendencies to the classic borderline profile, nevertheless is also not behaving with the paper-thin ego seen in such classic borderlines, and criticality is also less. Whereas the classic borderline person feels like "nothing," the more normally inclined borderline person can coexist with feeling terribly devalued along with feeling successful in one way or another, and, as a higher-functioning borderline type, can accomplish interesting personal goals.

CHAPTER SIXTEEN

The Depressed Style

As a detached personality type, the depressive character is one who is different from typical bipolar or manic-depressive types. These latter types show cyclical depression—now you see it (it is manic or depressed for a time), now you don't (it is either manic now while before it was depressed, or the other way around). The Depressive Style described is one in which such a person has had lasting effects of either a scolding and blame-seeking parent, or a parent who leaves a mark of permanent depression because of a tendency to convey, in a sometimes direct and hostile way, (even though sometimes indirect way), the threat of abandonment. Yet, in most of such cases, the primary caretaker may have, in fact, actually provided nurturing in the form of assuring physical safety for the child, as well as providing nourishment and shelter—and such a parent could have even shown affection.

However, the parent's severe attitude with respect to the expectation of obedience, compliance, and permission-seeking invariably can lead the child to feel unsure of what might happen if a display of disobedience were to be seen. In a derivative sense, the issue for the child turns into one of a fear of collision, and therefore such a person will be terrified of physical violence, or the threat of such violence, and generally will be fearful of any kind of possible interpersonal confrontation.

Because of the implicit threat of abandonment in the caretaker's severe demeanor, as well as other poor parenting effects on this depressed type, such a typically depressed person becomes increasingly self-absorbed (thinking primarily of one's needs), self-interested (in the survival sense), and thus, generally, self-preoccupied. Interestingly, the self-preoccupation contains a narcissistic component—but one that has the purpose of survival rather than aggrandizement. "Love me, but don't leave me," would be this person's mantra. The "*but*" in "but don't leave me," implies that there is an underlying threat that accompanies the promise of loving. The threat, of course, is that loving can go along with leaving. For example, and as a matter of fact, a person who exhibits this sort of depressed style becomes rather a minimalist: tends to minimize successes, and refuses to compete with others for fear of rejection, fear of being ignored, fear of being envied, and of course, because of the ultimate fears of collision, contention, confrontation, and abandonment. This is usually a lifelong dilemma: wanting to be detached but worrying about possibly being abandoned.

Therefore in this type self-esteem is always in a state of being recessed; that is, in practical terms, such a person must retain a full-proof stance of modesty. And in this sense of needing always to be modest, this sort of depressed type is usually self-effacing (never using self-aggrandizing phrases), deferential (bowing to the wishes and whims of others), and remaining opaquely on the edge of the shadow (on the penumbra), rather than being central or on center stage.

Insofar as relationships are concerned, persons who exhibit this sort of depressed style usually feel dissatisfied in relationships, and their partners similarly experience this dissatisfaction. A frequent complaint expressed by the partner is that the depressed person "finds it hard to give." Generally, this is so because such a depressed person is quite sensitive to rejection and therefore "giving" (as in affection) becomes the prelude to being more deeply involved. This means that the relationship will be more meaningful. In the face of fears of rejection and abandonment, this possibility of developing a deeper and more meaningful relationship is experienced by the depressed person as being potentially problematic. This means that if you get close, there is now a possibility that the partner can also leave, and even more, that if you indeed get close, you will by the very nature of your conflict need to comply completely with the other's wishes, thereby losing any bit of autonomy you may have achieved. It means feeling swallowed or engulfed by the relationship.

Yet, this depressed person also wishes for special treatment, and this wish becomes a lifelong yearning not to feel worried about such abandonment and rejection. Among the emotion-detached styles, it is this depressed personality that, despite the fears and anticipations of rejection, may still be able to manage a relationship, as for example, a marriage. However, the special need for such a person is for the other, the partner, to be understanding and able to withstand the absence of sufficient loving from the depressive one. The absence of sufficient loving would be a result of this depressed person's almost complete absorption with personal concerns—especially with the concerns of safety and security.

Paradoxically, despite the concern with safety and security, as well as the tension regarding rejection and abandonment, such a depressed style carries with it a tendency to criticize. It is essentially identification with the parent who was probably ambivalent about being a parent, and thus, even though such a parent provided basic needs, a critical foreboding attitude nevertheless may have been present in the initial parent-child relationship, and, as is usually the case, the child would identify with such a critical attitude and then later would imitate it.

The paradox is composed of being afraid of abandonment, and at the same time, courting rejection and abandonment by being consistently critical of the other. Because of this critical attitude, such a person also may appear to others to be an independent sort, who it would seem is immune to feeling either sympathy or empathy. Actually the opposite is true. Such persons usually over-identify with objects of pity such as wounded animals, or anyone who is rendered helpless.

Thus, this style of depressed personality is essentially emotionally detached because of the need to manage the challenge of a belief system that expects rejection and abandonment. The solution such a person creates with respect to the organization of personality, therefore, is not to be deeply involved, or if involved, not to display the involvement with any sort of special interest. This constitutes a rather subtle strategy that minimizes any serious probability of potential abandonment.

Case Examples

Case 1: Depressed Personality – A Symptom Sketch

A woman of thirty-seven was married to a man who adored her. He was smitten with her beauty, and no matter how deprived he was as a result of her under-response to him, his love for her enabled him to withstand her withholding personality. She was always somewhat down, and no matter how he tried to encourage her she could not relinquish her need to be withdrawn, also in the sense of feeling depressed.

This woman was prescribed antidepressant medication that helped her feel more animated, but which did not change her characteristic behavior of caution in interpersonal relationships exemplified by her typical under-response to the husband she claimed she loved. Her husband believed that she loved him, but insisted that because he knew her well, he could tell that she would be this way with anyone to whom she was married.

Her depressive stance was also evident in her low level of interest in sexual activity, and as a result, their marriage had gradually become more of a platonic affair even though he continued to be affectionate with her. She would never rebuff his affections but the problem was that she would never initiate similar affectionate displays toward him. Her husband correctly sensed that fundamentally his wife was an angry person underneath it all but her anger and dissatisfaction with life were cleverly concealed. This, of course was clinically quite astute because a hardcore psychological principle holds that where there is significant repressed anger there is no libido. That is to say that anger can anesthetize libidinous sexual feelings.

This woman's particular depressive symptom was traced to her early experience in her nuclear family in which her father was no match for his critical and controlling wife (her mother). Rather than showing depressive trends as a child, she instead became very compliant and modest in her responses. It was this modesty and compliance that gradually morphed into a depressive stance whereby she could achieve a certain amount of emotional security by keeping her distance in all relationships.

This woman was also an accomplished violinist, and her virtuosity invited many compliments from others, which she utilized in the service of appearing to be quite socially appropriate. She felt that her talent was useful in covering a host of sins. Yet, it was her lifelong strategy (though quite automatically derived) not to get too close for fear of inviting her partner to control her, and in this way she felt that in kind, she could avoid being involved with a controlling person.

Case 2: *The Depressed Personality*

A forty-two-year-old woman was usually moody, and had all sorts of complaints about things that bothered her in her marriage. She was not willing to be talkative upon awakening in the mornings and usually was even sullen. The cardinal symptom of her depressive personality was an oppositionalism that characterized almost everything she said or did. If her husband was happy about his raise at work, rather than share his joy, she might say that all he was interested in was money. It was this kind of variation in her oppositionalism that insinuated itself into just about every response she had.

Her husband would frequently complain about her inability to enjoy herself, but she would put up a strong defense to explain why she didn't like this or that. This was a person who could not be wrong about anything. Even when it was crystal clear that she was indeed wrong about something, she would try to argue it instead of simply admitting to having made an error. This sort of defensiveness drove a wedge into the sexual and affectional aspect to the marriage so that their marriage reached a point of a complete absence of physical contact.

This woman was so entirely self-absorbed with her personal concerns that the popular expression, "it's all about you," would have applied perfectly in describing her withdrawal, as well as her depressive moods. In addition, her sensitivity to possible rejection by others prompted her into a steady-state of anticipating criticism. This was a bit paranoid and her way of managing it was to defend against what she believed would be someone's criticism toward her by deciding to take the offense, and attack first. And this sort of response pattern was usually played out in her marriage and specifically against her husband—who, surprisingly, she insisted she loved. Otherwise her behavior was usually modest toward him and toward others as well.

This woman was quite introspective and intelligent but she felt she needed to protect herself by being hostile toward certain others, especially her husband, although not solely toward her husband. This hostility was occasionally expressed toward her husband especially in the morning hours when he wanted to talk and when she angrily insisted that she did not like to talk in the mornings.

Her history was such that she grew up with a mother who had great ambivalence about wanting to be a mother, and it seemed that this person's concerns and anxieties were linked to this ambivalent mother who because of her ambivalence was possibly also depressed, leading to a sense of feeling constrained about her role as a parent. This mother was inconsistent in her relationship to her daughter, and overall was also seen by many people as immature. The daughter's somewhat withdrawn quality was, in turn, seen as her way of never permitting anyone (husband included) to have the power to control her.

This woman gained reassurance through a kind of quasi-isolation (an emotionally detached style); that is, within her marriage and because of her chronic depressive disposition, the necessary distance she needed from her husband in order to maintain her emotional balance (and therefore sustain some peace of mind) was reflexively calibrated ultimately to position herself as a depressive personality.

The More Normally Inclined Depressed Style

The question is: Can a chronically depressive style be modified and become more normally inclined? The answer is a tentative *Yes.* If such a person has a certain skill that is utilized and that invites positive feedback with respect to this skill and about the productivity resulting from such a skill, then the person's sense of devaluation, anticipation of abandonment, defensive self-absorption, and even fears of collision can likely be moderated. This amounts to a shift in the culture of such a person's personality insofar as the traditions within that person's culture of personality can expand to include a newer tradition—that of receiving good news and not rejecting it. With time, this newer, *nondepressive tradition* can begin to compete rather effectively with the older depressive one.

The depressive person usually needs to be rescued and presents the picture of someone in distress or as being lost. It would seem that being successfully rescued would then open such a person to be more loving and giving. Yet, nothing could be further from the truth. This kind of person's self-effacing and minimalist psychological nature is usually quite strong, so that in any intimate relationship this person's rigidity will prevail. Logic of rescue will have no influence whatsoever. We are here dealing with strong needs not to be attached, not to give, never to be seen as central, given to oppositional impulses, all in a person with a rather fragile ego who because of this fragility will generally fight if accused of being wrong.

In the more normally inclined depressive style, however, the person may be able to express the above-mentioned skill (not automatically rejecting "the good news"), thereby having some pride in resisting the urge to be oppositional. This kind of development will usually loosen the strictures of the need for emotional detachment so that this type of person can begin to experiment with more smiling, more laughing, and even more risk-taking.

Because of original parental criticality, such a person necessarily has an inordinate identification with helplessness. With a partner who is understanding, loving, and loyal, and in addition is consistently present, the chronically depressive person has a chance to be more normal in a relationship, provided of course that such a person is also able to achieve responses that favor her or his productive skills and work—and importantly, is married to a partner with an inordinate capacity to suffer and wait it out.

CHAPTER SEVENTEEN

The Avoidant Style

THE PERSON WHO is diagnosed as an *avoidant personality* usually is quite self-protective insofar as guarding self-esteem becomes of chief concern. With respect to social engagement of any kind, fears of potential rejection and failure dominate this person's conscious expectations. Thus, the need for affection and acceptance is overshadowed by tension regarding this individual's certainty that social interaction will result in being scorned by others.

The obvious conflict such a person has concerns an understanding of potential relationships in which an implicit failure mechanism actually precludes any engagement of the relationship. Thus, such a person will believe that to perceive acceptance from another person becomes the prerequisite to entering the relationship. The problem is that because the avoidant person has an unshakable belief that rejection is what always will be forthcoming from another, then a possibility of acceptance will probably be accompanied by an "uh-oh." This *uh-oh* means that any potential interaction that could lead to a possible relationship is, from the outset, and for sure, considered doomed.

This kind of person can be emotionally easily hurt and because of this avoids such interaction. The result of this pattern of social avoidance is that such a person, therefore, ends up with few or no friends. In addition, because of this gloomy or pessimistic view of relationships, such a person avoids activities that mandate inter-personal contact. The avoidant personality also will shun social interaction in which there is even a remote chance of feeling fool-ish or anxious or humiliated. Thus, it becomes evident that the cardinal characteristic of this type of personality concerns the uniformly present fear of rejection from others. And this kind of fear insinuates itself in all spheres of the person's life including in the person's fantasy life as well as in the operation of emotions within the personality, and finally generally in all of the individual's behavior.

In addition, another interesting facet of this person's conflict concerns the dilemma that such individuals frequently have in which social affiliations and acceptance from others can be desired, but that the quest for such unconditional acceptance from others in the face of a pessimism and certain expectation of rejection creates the mandate for social isolation. In this sense, the upshot of the effects of this personality style is that social withdrawal assures a distancing in relationships and even causes an extremely cautious approach to vocational choices and functioning.

Because of the avoidant impulse as well as the social pessimism that such an avoidant type necessarily lives with, a devaluation of the self becomes natural to experience. In other words every-thing positive is attributed to the other person while expectation that the other will be justifiably rejecting means that everything negative is attributed to the self. In this sense, a social inhibition begins to dominate the person's life and this inhibiting orienta-tion leads to distancing behaviors that actually begin to generate feelings of emotional security simply because being socially iso-lated precludes being rejected.

Along with this isolative tendency, a system of rationalizations (excuses and reasons) is developed to justify such avoidant behav-ior along with subsequent social isolation. These rationalizations then justify such a person's strategy of always being cautious in potential interpersonal relationships, so that to err on the cautious side becomes the habitual gamble. Such caution gradually becomes pervasive so that the person usually will develop an entire variety of risk-averse attitudes. Of course in extended periods of isolation, and despite the comfort it gives such a person, nevertheless depressive feelings and frustration along with anger become generated and ultimately begin to affect such an individual with feelings of inertia and passivity in a way that then dominates the person's life.

Case Examples

Case 1: Avoidant Personality– A Symptom Sketch

A twenty-two-year-old young man was referred for psychotherapy consultation because his father could no longer abide his reclusive and odd behavior. He lived in an apartment that his parents had helped subsidize. His mother was a passive woman who worked as a seamstress so that it was his father as well as both of his sisters who had the greatest say in raising him. His father had been on disability income for a decade because of a factory accident that left him partially blind in one eye and practically without hearing. Despite this condition of reduced sensory input, he was apparently able to handle the household chores and ostensibly supervise his son and both of his daughters. Both of these daughters (who were quite older than the twenty-two-year old) had left home by the time he was thirteen, and as was reported they said, "for good reasons."

In the psychotherapy consultation, this young man described his father as paranoid. He said his father's disturbance consisted of suspicions that the neighbors were harboring, as the father said, "wicked ideas" about him. His father would also peek through the peephole in their apartment door in order to check the common public hallway, and when the coast was clear, he would roam these hallways and with his ear up against a neighbor's door would try to listen to any conversation that was occurring inside the neighbor's apartment—an act this patient said that was bizarre because his father was actually quite hard of hearing. The father also engaged in other paranoidlike behaviors, and the patient stated that it was such bizarre behavior that drove his sisters to leave and that enabled him to leave as well. When he turned eighteen, his sisters encouraged him to get a job, and with their help and his parents' subsidy, he was able to afford a studio apartment.

As a result of his father's incessant snooping and suspiciousness, this man confessed to being quite ashamed and awkward during his formative years especially with respect to meeting anyone in their apartment building. He even would avoid taking the elevator to their third-floor apartment and rather climbed the stairs in order to avoid contact with anyone. This kind of behavior generalized itself, and he reported that he was also quite hermitlike throughout grammar school as well as high school. He said that most people knew about his father's strange behavior and it was that kind of public knowledge that actually gave this patient an unrelenting sense that he wanted always to hide.

It was this particular symptom of a heightened focus of "hiding" that constituted the major personality characteristic this young man displayed especially since he was relieved when alone in his apartment. His conflict expressed in the therapy work was that he craved the company of friends; but because he felt terribly awkward in social situations, he was always worried about rejection.

In this kind of isolation, this young man's fantasy life began to be similar to his father's about how others were not friendly to him. It was beginning to be a case of *une folie a deux* (double insanity—figuratively speaking): that two people can share the same pathology.

Again, however, the main issue in the diagnosis regarding this avoidant personality style was that the reclusive behavior of this young man afforded him relief of tension and at least in the short run, offered him solitude and refuge.

Case 2: The Avoidant Personality

A fifty-year-old woman was a librarian for a philanthropic foundation. She had been at that job for almost twenty-five years. She was a single woman who lived on the ground floor of an apartment building. It was her habit never to speak to anyone entering or leaving the building, and her neighbors generally felt she was "a bit off."

Her job was ideal since she could work in an environment wherein hardly anyone was around, and it was her job to care for the archives and handle the correspondences of the organization. In this respect, she was *an isolate* where she lived, and somewhat isolated even in her work life. She noted that she was a shy person all of her life, and never had boyfriends. She also had never experienced sexual intimacy and denied even masturbating. Everything about this woman was surrounded with issues regarding clear-cut avoidance behavior, social isolation, and solitary living.

Her problem occurred when the foundation for which she worked acquired a new president, and this person was a demanding task-master who from time to time was critical in his comments and unfriendly in his tone. Of course this woman responded to such an approach with disdain but with a kind of certainty that the president was right about her and that he had uncovered her true incompetence. Her own self-devaluation fed directly into this president's rather icy and inhospitable approach, and because of this woman's basic underlying avoidant-personality organization, she made it two against one; she had his rejecting vote as far as her work was concerned, and because of her own self-devaluing stance, agreed with him. That was the two against one. To have another person as the enemy is one thing; but for you to be your own enemy is quite another!

Her solution was to decide to resign from her job. But she didn't. Fortunately the president lasted a short time and was replaced by a friendlier person who actually appreciated this woman's work, and his acceptance of her became also a lifeline to her. For example, whereas in the past she would be terribly afraid of saying an incorrect thing or something inappropriate, she was now less tense about talking. In addition, her usual pessimism and social avoidance was also attenuated so that she looked forward to going to work even though she maintained a kind of neutrality with this new president.

The More Normally Inclined Avoidant Style

A more normally inclined avoidant style occurs when the avoidant type is part of a social context in which other members of the context are friendly and accepting. This was the case with the woman in the above case illustration, particularly when the new friendly president was appointed. In that situation, fears of certain rejection, a classic guardedness of self-esteem, and an overall thin skin, were attenuated so that the woman's sense of self-devaluation correspondingly was also attenuated. Therefore, as an avoidant personality, after the new president entered the picture, she became somewhat more normally inclined and her relief from tension and anxiety no longer required her to seek the isolation and solitary life of existing solely in her apartment. She could actually consider the possibility of having friends. Her newly found acceptance from this new director of the foundation essentially short-circuited more intense feelings of depression, frustration, anger, inertia, and passivity—characteristics that would ordinarily comprise a cluster of difficult emotions. In a totally accepting environment, such feelings and consequent behavior were significantly challenged.

In this respect, although this person remained quite fixed as an avoidant personality, nevertheless circumstance played an important part in forcing her to face the fact that she was accepted by one and all. Facing this fact and acting accordingly was the primary issue in inclining this woman to be a more normal avoidant type and therefore to feel as though she had friends. It made for a measure of greater ease and some happiness.

Conclusion

IN THIS BOOK an attempt is made to identify and consolidate salient considerations in the understanding of personality development and personality type and style. We have considered that personality is psycho-mechanically wired in the same way for all people and is therefore species-specific. That is, our personality mechanisms are all the same. Our differences reside in personality styles and depend upon how such mechanisms work to configure varieties of personalities and varieties of personality-trait patterns of behavior. Our contribution here is that because of our categorization the vast amount of personality data is organized into more manageable and parsimonious arrangements of personality types so that their correspondence one to the other is likewise more understandable, and very importantly seems to give us access to the patterns within the psyche: within the psychological and emotional components of the psyche (mind).

The enormous variety of diagnostic types creates confusion in trying to see how one diagnostic personality configuration relates to another or if, in fact, they do relate one to the other. Distilled in order to induce a coherence of all of these factors is the powerful·organizing principle concerning how emotion is managed in the personality. As it turns out, this organizing principle permits a basic complement of personality types to be arranged so that one can then see how they relate one to the other. In a word, a person can identify himself or herself and then understand the underpinnings that conspired and ultimately amalgamated to form their particular brand or personality style.

These components of the personality that formed around the basic idea of how emotion is managed in the personality includes the issues of: the importance of memory in the face of repressive forces; the person's wish-system and its drive toward gratification; the appearance of symptoms based upon thwarted wishes; the importance of understanding the urge of impulses; the more important issue of how controls can tame the impulses (and the implications that derive should such control fail); and the system of defense mechanisms that are designed to fortify one's personality configuration with respect to type and style.

Ultimately, the importance of understanding the make-up of the personality is to facilitate the person's ability to recognize where the struggle is located in order to better overcome conflicts and to seek more adaptive functioning—the kind of functioning that permits one to aspire and to implement activity that is directed and targeted to goals that would be more in the person's best interest. In this sense, we have presented material to show how each of the diagnostic styles perhaps may exist in a more normally inclined portrayal.

Implicit in all is the notion that to struggle with important goals—even within the larger struggle of working-through self-defeating personality habits or styles—can be one of the only dignities and can elevate one's sense of mastery in life.

In this book is thus displayed how the wiring of personality traits are etched and therefore seemingly engraved in permanent position. But we also know that personality can be altered and that people can work on problems in a way that has the potential to elevate the person by promoting patterns of personality that, again, are more in the person's interest, simultaneously assisting in the receding of those personality traits that are rather not in the person's interests. The question is: How do we do that? How do we change personality?

How Does Personality Change? How Can It Re-form?

Despite the fact that the human personality may be a most-resistant force, nevertheless theoretically it is thought to be possible to change personality. There has been a way of thinking about it all that confirms that this particular modality of implementing the approach to changing personality has actually proved even stronger than the strength of the so-called permanence of personality-trait configurations themselves.

Furthermore, aspects of personality can definitely change just as traditions in culture change. This means that sometimes there are certain traditions in any culture that no longer are best for that culture, and the society introduces newer behavior patterns and traditions that become assimilated into the general society. This newer form in the culture gives it a somewhat different cast to the configuration of the collective cultural personality. The same is true for the traditions of the culture of any individual's personality. Such traditions of the personality are really response inclinations, or reflexive responses, and/or patterns of responses. When such patterns are no longer positive or in the best interest of the person, newer patterns can be introduced so that a newer tradition in the culture of that person's personality begins to effectively compete with the older, less-valuable tradition.

This way of thinking about personality change is a general underpinning to the working out of a person's symptoms and conflicts. It is such symptoms and conflicts that identify the person in a certain familiar fashion to others, and this identifying familiarity of someone's personality becomes that person's style or signature. Changing such persona (despite its strength), is what re-forming or enhancing personality is all about, so that conflicts and symptoms can be successfully challenged.

However, one problem that exists in the formation of symptoms and conflicts concerns the fact that a symptom can become something akin to a personality trait so that as *a trait,* the symptom becomes even more resistant to change.

Why Does the Symptom Become a Symptom-trait?

Here is the issue of anger again. The problem is that one's psyche (that property of the mind that keeps personality working) can be understood as having a certain measure of strength, of density, of resilience, and so forth. As such, the psyche can absorb all sorts of emotional experience and can be able to contain and organize this emotional experience. In some cases, however, the psyche will experience certain emotional input as onerous enough so that a strong possibility exists that the psyche will extrude it—throw it out, exile it.

In the case of anger and its intrinsic relation to symptoms, following are the criteria by which the psyche determines what stays and what goes:

Magnitude—This means that if the magnitude of the anger covers the entire psyche it can threaten to take over and, because of its volume, undo all of the personality organization that the psyche has provided. In such a case the psyche will want it out.

Intensity—This means that if the intensity or severity of the anger is too great, the psyche will experience it as threatening to its integrity and again feel it must extirpate it—cut it out.

Depth—This means that if the anger threatens to penetrate to the core of the psyche, it will be categorically expostulated from the psyche because of its possible devastating effects to the personality.

Duration—This means that if the anger has existed for a long time it can have the effect of eroding the resilience of the psyche, and for this reason it will also be considered a candidate for exclusion.

Thus, when a psychological/emotional symptom contains all the features of such anger implosion, the symptom will not be permitted to exist in the domain of the psyche where psychological/emotional symptoms usually reside. Rather, when these onerous criteria for the exclusion of symptoms exist the psyche will experience the threat and, as a result, then dispatch such a symptom to the domain relegated to personality-traits and out of the domain of the psyche reserved for typical symptoms. In such a case, the symptom becomes *a symptom-trait.* A symptom-trait simply means an attitude with a behavioral capacity.

With respect to treating and trying to cure the symptom-as-trait, the person will need to dilute his or her anger in order for this symptom-trait to be treated more as a typical symptom. Thus, the *magnitude, intensity,* and *depth* of the anger will need to be at least modulated. In such a case, the issue of *duration* of the anger becomes ever so gradually less of an issue.

To Understand What Anger Does and How It Works

The simple matter is that no symptom can exist unless anger toward a specific person has been repressed. In typical symptoms, just about all of the anger has been repressed so that the therapist's task is to help the patient get in touch with the anger and then try to identify *the who* toward whom the anger had been intended. When both of these conditions are satisfied, that is, getting in touch with the anger and successfully rounding up the usual suspects of the patient's life in order to identify *the who* who was the person in the first place responsible for thwarting the subject's wish, at that point, the symptom is very likely to lift and the subject can be free of it. It is in this sense that consciousness becomes curative: what becomes conscious is the deepest repressed anger toward a particular person.

The consideration of treating a symptom-trait reveals that the person who is so troubled with such a symptom-trait may in fact be experiencing a measure of the anger. The trick here is in the realization that there is something basically hidden almost in plain sight: That is, that despite the fact that some anger may be overtly displayed, all of it tends to obscure the point that in addition to this surfaced, conscious display of anger, there exists another layer of anger that is buried in the unconscious, repressed as it were, so that the subject (the person with the symptom) does not even know it is there. This is the nexus of the problem because such underlying anger is like a furnace that needs constant stoking. The way it is stoked becomes the crux of the problem. An anger furnace is always hungry for more fuel. When this occurs, the person will seek additional reasons to be angry at *the who*—the person toward whom the anger was initially directed.

When the unconscious anger-furnace is extinguished, and this deepest anger toward *the who* becomes conscious, then the symptom that was plaguing the person is very likely to disappear instantly, especially if the person does something related to the original wish. The operative term is *does*. The doing of something related to the person's original wish, which was initially thwarted by *the who,* is what needs to be done.

With these considerations in mind concerning the change-possibility in one's personality—especially with respect to habitual personality-trait responses as well as in the operation of symptoms—the question can be asked: How can personality patterns, those world-class hardest substances, re-form?

The answer is by way of knowing *Personality: How It Forms* (and how it can re-form).

Glossary

More on the State of the Personality

Summary Statement Regarding Chapters 6 to17

In these twelve chapters, basic styles of the personality were delineated. It needs to be remembered that these are hypothetically pure styles, but that any person's particular style is usually not pure in the sense of being an absolute replica of any one of these twelve definitive personality configurations. Therefore, it is most likely the case that trying to find one's own personality among the twelve described here will be more fruitful when it is realized that in life most people adapt in ways that make it possible to have a mixed picture rather than any absolute one.

For example, it is very likely that someone can be obsessive and have compulsive features that also contain passive-aggressive factors of the personality as well as dependent characteristics. In this sense, it is perfectly clear that anyone trying to locate who they are by referring to the descriptions of the basic personalities described in chapters 6 to 17, will need to locate various features of their own personality which can probably be identified by searching each of the twelve chapters, and then probing particular traits that seem to resemble those that are familiar, and that the searcher can claim as resembling a self-trait.

A key of course to finding who you are is to understand that we all orient ourselves according to how we manage our emotions as well as our interpersonal relationships. And in this respect, each person needs to ask: Am I more or less an emotion-controlled person, or an emotion-dyscontrolled person? Am I an emotion-attached person, or an emotion-detached person? Am I emotion-controlled and as well, emotion-attached, or am I emotion-controlled and as well, emotion-detached? Am I emotion-dyscontrolled and as well, emotion-attached, or emotion-dyscontrolled and as well, emotion-detached?

If one is able to identify their predilections with respect to how they manage their emotions (as well as their interpersonal relationships) by searching through chapters 6 to 17, it will be relatively easy to notice those traits that seem familiar and then to form a constellation of personality traits that one has identified within these chapters, which in toto will comprise that person's personality style and overall personality configuration. It will constitute one's personality profile.

A special note regarding how one finds the particular personality style that fits. The question becomes: Is there anything else I should know about forming this personality profile?

The answer to this question is: Yes, there are other things to know. What are these other things? What needs to be added here are other diagnostic descriptions that we have not covered in the twelve basic dispositional styles. However, it is proposed that the twelve styles that we have covered comprise a fairly approximate amalgam of basic types onto which can be layered additional features, such as transitory symptoms, mood disorders, and even more-serious diagnoses such as schizophrenia, bipolar disorder, even disorders associated with brain trauma or genetic anomalies.

What "the Nervous Breakdown" Really Means

What we have done here by listing the twelve basic styles is to focus on habitual patterns of behavior that are not usually considered psychotic (either schizophrenic or severely disturbed affectively [emotionally]). Yet, we also know that many people are psychotic (afflicted with terrible disturbances of thinking [that is, schizophrenia], or severe disturbances of mood [that is, manic-depressive]). This is what is actually meant by the popular phrase *nervous breakdown*. It refers to the two classifications of psychosis (the state of one's being whereby the person's testing of reality and consequent judgment is rendered as cognitively and/or emotionally unhinged, preposterous, or nonsensical). Such disturbance is usually classified either as a thinking disorder, as in schizophrenia, or as an affective disorder, as in manic-depressive or bipolar/psychotic.

In this respect of the appearance in individual expression of these more severe phenomena seen in a person's disturbance, the following listing comprises a sample of such additional categories of personality variation; some more severe, some less, but which do affect personality organization and that may be attached to basic personality-style configurations presented in chapters 6 to 17.

These fill out the glossary of important terms in the understanding of personality styles and types.

Other Diagnoses of the Glossary Samples of More Severe Disorders Regarding Affect (Emotion)

DEPRESSION

The depressive style that we have considered here is one that has a chronic tinge to it and characterizes the entire personality with a quality that essentially contains a cluster of traits such as pessimism, modesty, shyness, "down mood" such as in gloominess, "dispiritatiousness," and, generally speaking, with a kind of dismal outlook. It is the style of a person who is somewhat devitalized and enervated. This more severe depression contains extreme symptoms such as sleep and eating disturbance, distractability in thinking and concentration, terrible energy deficiency, certainty of worthlessness, and in the even more disturbed aspects of such a depressive disorder of mood, hallucinations as well as delusions may be seen. Such a person can also be suicidal.

MANIC

This particular form of mania contains severe dyscontrol of emotion and behavior that reveals enormous expenditure of energy in which such a person can be involved in a spate of projects and despite this, such a person may only need a minimal amount of sleep. This person therefore will be endlessly expansive and even irritable, and there will also be tremendous pressure to talk. A flight of ideas is also typical and such a person can become compulsively and inappropriately engaged in "buying" (spending) ventures, can disregard pain, and will utilize an overabundance of compensatory behaviors that justify a grandiose fantasy life. Theoretically, all of it is designed in the personality to ward off underlying depression by being grandiose and self-aggrandizing, and all of it presumably acts as a defense against a most serious potential depression.

BIPOLAR

This is analogous to manic-depressive disorder in which manic and depressive moods alternate. Pressured speech, overall increased activity, restlessness, flight of ideas (ideas running from one to the other and suddenly so), grandiosity, and distractability are some of the issues afflicting such a person. In addition, in severe cases, violence becomes the most derivative action of this person's need to express the impulse that is at the core of impatience, dissatisfaction, and the extreme inability to tolerate frustration.

CYCLOTHYMIA

Here, the person expresses depressed mood alternating with emotional excitement. When the person is depressed, motoric activity is slowed and when the person is excited, a hypomanic quality (somewhat less than fully manic) will appear in the form of grandiosity, optimism, euphoria, and overall expansiveness.

DYSTHYMIA

This is less severe than a full-blown depression, and no excitement occurs. It is related to a host of other diagnostic categories previously utilized by clinicians in an attempt to categorize such a state accurately. Some of these former designations include depressive neurosis, depressive reaction, exogenous depression, and reactive depression. These are all disturbances in "pleasure" in which the person cannot seem to find happiness or relief from tension within "the down mood." However, sometimes the dysthymia with respect to depressive mood was labeled *reactive depression* since the depression apparently was designed in the personality to allay anxiety. For example, a depression that was caused by the death of a loved one would be considered "reactive" because it enabled the sufferer not to feel the pain of the anxiety. Such a person with dysthymia is also pervasively pessimistic and generally feels terribly inadequate. Avoidance of social interaction is also typical with such a mood.

AGITATED DEPRESSION

Here, the person encounters situations that generate sudden and terrible agitation, irritability, impatience, dissatisfaction, anxiety, impulsivity, restlessness, insomnia, and a host of other phenomena that create discomforts. Covert hostility is also seen because the agitation is characterized by terribly angry feelings, and the person will be in a state in which a perpetual sense of feeling a so-called wrongness exists.

Samples of Severe Disorders Regarding "Thinking Disturbance"

Within the psychotic or extremely disturbed variants of schizophrenia (the thinking disorders), there has been an evolution in the psychiatric science of categorization. For many years, the following tetrad of disorders were the standard understanding of how such categories, with respect to symptomatology, were arranged. As far as schizophrenia, these were:

THE SIMPLE TYPE

Flattened affect, an insidious process of withdrawal from the world (ending in profound isolation that usually leads the person into a so-called autistic state), and a minimal response to enjoyment or warmth in relationships characterize such behavior.

THE HEBEPHRENIC TYPE

Silliness, inappropriate giggling, childish embarrassment, and inappropriate affect generally characterize such behavior.

THE CATATONIC TYPE

The extreme polarity here concerns the person fluctuating between extreme withdrawal and extreme excitement. In the withdrawn state, the person will become fixed in one position and may not move at all for a long period of time. The skin will acquire what is known as "a waxy flexibility." Stupor or mutism accompanies this behavior. When in the excited stage, a so-called catatonic excitement can produce a destructive person who can be violent.

THE PARANOID TYPE

Delusions of either grandiosity or persecution characterize this person's state. Hallucinations also may be seen. Jealousy and criticality are also typical.

Additional Categories of "Thinking Disorders" (Schizophrenia)

THE DISORGANIZED TYPE

This diagnostic syndrome contains some incoherence in language expression—emotional disturbance with respect to inconsistent expression of emotion—although with an absence of the posturing that would be seen in the catatonic person.

THE PSEUDONEUROTIC TYPE

This is a former type that was clinically useful but did not last in the psychiatric-categorization system *(nosology)*. Yet, clinicians still refer to it because it is seen clinically with patients. Here the patient displays a host of nonpsychotic behaviors and thinking, although it is believed that because of the classic evidence of a pervasive pan-anxiety (covering all of the arenas of the person's life), that therefore an underlying psychotic personality organization is what is causing the permeating anxiety.

THE SCHIZOAFFECTIVE TYPE

Here, a mixture of schizophrenic thinking and affective psychotic symptoms join. The person will show cognitive disturbance as well as affect disturbance with delusions and hallucinations.

Additional Categories of Anxiety and Neurotic States (Non-psychotic)

THE PANIC STATE

Characterized by periods of intense dread and may include dizziness, fainting, heart palpitations, sweating, and nausea. This is much more severe than an average anxiety condition.

THE GENERALIZED ANXIETY STATE

Contains an experience of "free-floating anxiety" including symptoms of fearful anticipations, sleep difficulty, facial strain, muscle aching, and perhaps hyperventilation that can cause a sense of possibly losing consciousness.

THE POSTTRAUMATIC STRESS STATE

Involves acute and especially delayed types of terror reactions to traumatic and catastrophic previous experiences. Anxiety is generated to this experience that contains flashbacks and nightmares. Such difficulty results in a host of symptoms including reduced ability to concentrate and memory dysfunction.

THE BODY DYSMORPHIC STATE

The person will focus on a body part as being imperfect. This can reach the level of delusion and it is thought that such a person's presumed physical imperfection is a displacement of a sense of personal inadequacy. This presumed inadequacy feeling can be related to experiences in childhood of not being confident in expressing assertive feelings and generally seeing the self as not good enough; and/or the disorder itself can be a self-devaluation based upon anger toward another person that is rather self-directed.

THE CONVERSION STATE

A physical change can take place in the form of symptoms that create tunnel vision, glove anesthesia, or even paralysis of limbs. This is akin to what was formerly called *the hysteric reaction.*

THE HYPOCHONDRIACAL STATE

Here the person is over-concerned with bodily functions and exaggerates possible harm that can result from not continuously checking with the doctor. Phantom symptoms may even appear and the person is constantly scanning the self, and inevitably finding that something somewhere on the body is problematic. The person will always feel re-empowered when the medical findings deem the patient to be fine and not at all sick.

THE SOMATIZATION STATE

Actual physical impairments occur but they are definitely psychologically based. These can include swallowing problems, fainting, muscle weakness, and a general inability to experience pleasure.

THE SOMATOFORM PAIN STATE

The person complains of pain in the body located in a variety of places. No organic basis is found for such complaints although there is little doubt that the person actually experiences such pain.

DISSOCIATIVE IDENTITY DISORDER

Formerly called *multiple personality* and *split personality,* this person will show a minimum of three distinct personalities: one is the host (the everyday person), a second is the aggressive person, and a third is the sexual one. As it works, the alternate personalities (aggressive and sexual) know of the presence of one another and of the host, whereas the host ostensibly is not aware of the other two.

THE PSYCHOGENIC FUGUE STATE

The person's main personality goes into a kind of hibernation (is suppressed or dissociated) and therefore becomes inaccessible to consciousness. Thus, conscious identity is temporarily lost. New identity features are acquired by such a person in this state, and these new features are very different than the person's true features of identity.

THE PSYCHOGENIC AMNESIC STATE

A loss of memory is typical here and can usually be related to a stressor in the person's life. It can appear suddenly and disappear just as quickly. In this state, the memory block eliminates the anxiety and tension associated with the stressor.

THE DEPERSONALIZATION STATE

Here there is a disorientation and profound alteration in the sense of self, as if the person is in a dreamlike state. Self-identity is temporarily blurred. It causes anyone with such an experience to feel crazy and frightened. It is usually not permanent.

Glossary

Part 1 (The Wiring of the Personality) and

Part 2 (The Basic Personality Styles)

Acting-out – Doing something rather than knowing or realizing something. The doing is usually something that is delinquent and/or self-defeating. Designed in the psyche to avoid tension.

Acting-in – Internalizing the anxiety so that the symptom attacks the self (as for example in the pain of migraine headaches).

Action-orientation – Tendency of the person to want to be in modes of "doing" such as in initiating behavior or moving about.

Anxiety—Signals more serious stress than simple general tension. Seen also to be a function of radiating anger located in the unconscious. The presence of anxiety has traditionally been a prerequisite for an existing diagnosis of neurosis.

Character trait – Equivalent to personality trait, implying consistent behavioral patterns

Cognitive operations—Use of intellect, judgment, thinking, attention to detail, memory, concentration, and planning ability are examples of facets of cognitive operations.

Compliance-building – Learning limits; learning to obey rules.

Consciousness – Being aware.

Controls – Utilizing cognitive, ego functions, defense mechanisms, character traits, fantasy, and fear, for the control of anxiety and impulses, and to enable a delay of gratification.

Counterphobic – A clinical term meaning that a fear is responded to by running toward the object of the fear rather than away from it.

Death instinct – An alternative Freudian definition of needing to reduce tension to zero.

Defenses – Mechanisms of the personality designed to manage emotion and help in the formation of personality traits.

Defenses to manage character-trait patterns – These include: identification, internalization, projective-identification, splitting, symbolization, and turning against the self.

Defenses to manage transitory emotion – compartmentalization, denial, displacement, intellectualization, isolation, projection, rationalization, reaction-formation, regression, repression, sublimation, and undoing.

Delusion – A false belief to the extent of it being outlandish.

Disempowerment – Helplessness; without power.

Displacement – A defense mechanism that searches for substitute people toward whom to direct hostility rather than directing the hostility to an originally targeted person.

Emotion-attached – Those personality types or styles where the person feels best if attached to someone as though to be an assistant.

Emotion-controlled – Those personality types or styles in which the person feels better when able to control emotion.

Emotion-detached – Those personality types or styles where the person feels best if not attached to anyone, as though completely free or able to be separate.

Emotion-dyscontrolled – Those personality types or styles in which the person feels better when emotion can be free and not controlled or restricted.

Identification – Internal dispositions as well as behavior are essentially imitated by the child who, by virtue of observation of, and experience with the parents, affects the child's overall developing personality.

Impulses – Strong inclinations of the personality such as the potential for emotional arousal as well as energized products of the psyche such as sexuality and aggression.

Internalization – A mechanism of the psyche based on the foundation of "identification" whereby the child is subject to an imprinting of parental values.

Personality profile – Essentially a listing of an individual's personality characteristics.

Personality-trait patterns – A series of typical responses a person has that combine to form predictable behavior of that person insofar as such a pattern becomes part of the person's personality signature.

Plasticity of personality – The mind's (psyche's) way of creating and operating mechanisms in the personality in order to manage tensions better.

Pleasure principle – The concept that reveals the person's desire to always seek pleasure. The person's wish is the pleasure principle's chief representative.

Projection – A defense-mechanism to point criticism toward another for some quality that the person doing the pointing does not want to see in the self.

Psyche – That part of the mind that mediates emotion and defenses and controls the balance between impulses and controls of the personality. The psyche has the ability to calibrate the degree to which feelings and ideas are consigned to the unconscious. The psyche is also "the furnace" (container) in which symptoms are formed.

Rationalization – A defense mechanism whereby one gives oneself reasons or excuses for one's behavior or motivation.

Repressed – Pushed into the unconscious mind and out of awareness.

Somatized anxiety – Anxiety transferred into some physical bodily symptom.

Submissive acquiescence – Agreeing to be secondary in a relationship.

Symptom – Reaction of the personality that emotionally grips the person so that the individual cannot really stop the reaction. A symptom is formed when anger toward a particular (specific) person is repressed (pushed down into the unconscious mind) so that the symptom then represents the person's wish that was initially blocked by that other person. Now the individual has the wish gratified, but only in the mind and then played-out in the form of a symptom (for example, a fear of heights, or a thought you cannot shake, or a repetitive checking of the locks on your door at night).

Tension – Feeling of opposing forces stressing the person.

Thin-ego – A person who has a thin-ego is supersensitive to anything that feels bothersome. Such a person can fall apart or feel explosive at the slightest distress.

Thwarted wish – A wish that is blocked by a specific person.

Transitory emotions – Emotions that quickly come and go. Examples include anger, fear, joy, sorrow, acceptance, disgust, anticipation, surprise.

Emotion-controlled Styles
(To control anxiety by controlling emotion)

Obsessive-compulsive Style – Such an individual is perfectionistic, busy working, and uses intellectualized defenses. The person rationalizes decisions and always needs to be right. Rumination in thinking is prevalent and the person frequently needs to act out the rumination (for example, checking the lock on the door).

Paranoid Style – Such a person is highly critical toward others as a way of keeping any criticism away from the self. Thus, all is wrong in the world—out there—but not within. Such a person is frequently jealous of others, is stubborn, usually blames others, doesn't accept things easily, and is rather suspicious. He or she uses projection as a main defense mechanism.

Schizoid Style – This is a nonschizophrenic person who nevertheless is socially detached, aloof, and therefore who avoids close relationships. Such a person leads a solitary social life but whose fantasy life is frequently animated with revenge themes. Here, emotion is suppressed.

Emotion-dyscontrolled Styles
(To control anxiety by keeping emotion uncontrolled)

Histrionic Style – Shows excessive emotionality. Is dramatic in the display of behavior. Makes exaggerated claims of social bonding with others. Immature. This person has difficulty being alone and finds it difficult to delay gratification. Needs to be constantly romantic. Is a dependent person who is soaked with personal wishes. This is a person who uses the defense of denial so that only wishes are accepted and other material rejected. A strong fantasy life is typical with sexual and seductive themes dominating the psyche. This is a highly suggestible person who can be easily hypnotized.

Narcissistic Style – Feels overly entitled but very insecure underneath. Entirely compensatory and therefore engaged in aggrandized fantasies of power and success. Achievements are also exaggerated because the person seeks adoration. Such a person is exhibitionistic but also envious and supersensitive to criticism.

Psychopathic Style – An antisocial person with an absence of concern about the boundaries of others. Always needs to gain advantage. Delinquent behavior is usual and includes fighting, stealing, lying, and promiscuity. Poor judgment is seen. There is insufficiency of conscience, and an absence of guilt and remorse. This person's inner life is presumably quite impoverished and therefore it is a person who needs endless external stimulation to make up for the nature of such a limited inner life.

Emotion-attached Styles
(To control anxiety by keeping emotion mild
and arranging for attached/compliant behavior)

Dependent Style – The person craves support and becomes submissive. Avoids responsibility. Sensitive to criticism. Needs constant reassurance. Anger needs to be controlled.

Inadequate Style – The person under-responds in all aspects of life although the IQ may remain adequate or even high. This person is dependent and needs to be emotionally attached to the caregiver. Inferiority feelings prevail and self-esteem is typically low. This individual is usually socially timid and is frequently risk-averse. Poor judgment is seen.

Passive-aggressive Style – This is a person who pays homage to the caretaker or dominant person, simultaneously expressing anger and dissatisfaction. The dissatisfaction or hostility is conveyed in an ostensibly innocent manner, and an apology always follows. Sometimes the passive-aggressive behavior takes a passive form, sometimes an aggressive form, and sometimes a dependent form. The person's anger is generated because of the incessant nature of underlying dependency that breeds resentment and constitutes the motive for frustrating the authority figure. For example, such frustration of the authority figure frequently occurs through behavior of procrastination and forgetting to do things.

Separation Anxiety – Dread of separating from the caregiver so that traits of cooperation, passivity, and compliance become typical. Synonymous with abandonment fears.

Emotion-detached Styles
(Designed to reduce tension by keeping the person emotionally detached and free of social entanglements)

Avoidant Style —This is a person who needs to protect a sense of self-esteem and does so by becoming avoidant. It is a person always worried about rejection from others and as a result becomes socially withdrawn. The person anticipates failure of relationships, which invokes a fear of humiliation. Pessimism is a chief trait here to the extent that positive qualities are attributed to others whereas negative qualities are directed to the self. Such a person eventually becomes chronically risk-averse.

Borderline Style —Such a person is characteristically emotionally unstable. This person consistently and serially idealizes (worships) others, but then also devalues these others. Consistency is therefore problematic. The underlying problem is one of fear of abandonment and an unstable sense of self. Drug usage, self-mutilation, and suicidal gestures are typically seen. Low frustration tolerance and temper tantrums are also typical, and vocational success becomes difficult to achieve.

Depressed Style —In contrast to manic-depressive or bipolar difficulty, this type of person is afflicted with a more long-standing or chronic depressive mood. Such a person becomes inconsistent and experiences a fear of collisions. This means that such a person is afraid of interpersonal contact and anticipates rejection. A sense or pattern of self-absorption becomes typical and the presumed underlying cause of this pattern refers to a history with a severe and critical parent who demanded compliance "or else." The *or else* implies that abandonment is the ultimate punishment for defiance. Such a person also refuses to compete for fear of upsetting the other and causing an interpersonal confrontation. Modesty is the default condition since it usually precludes the possibility of rejection by the other person. Self-effacing behavior and deference also become typical. Here, close relationships imply danger of engulfment, and yet the individual can be critical as an identification with the critical parent, so that even in a personal relationship such a person has trouble giving (being lovingly demonstrative). This person identifies with wounded animals.

Triad of Conditions —Seen in the borderline personality. It is composed of a typical trait-pattern of pan-anxiety, pan-sexuality, and pan-defensiveness. It means that anxiety, sexuality, and defensiveness pervade (cover) the personality.